*The Practical Sailor Library*
# Volume II •
# Commissioning and
# Decommissioning

# Commissioning and Decommissioning

*Preparing a New Boat/*
*Seasonal Launching and Layup*

Edited by Keith Lawrence

ISBN: 1-879620-33-2

Printed in the United States of America by The Ovid Bell Press, Fulton, Missouri

# Acknowledgments

Over the years, *The Practical Sailor* and *Better Boat* have benefitted from a dedicated staff and knowledgeable contributing editors, from the advice of numerous marine industry professions, and from the input and experience of thousands of loyal readers. In addition to extending our thanks to all of these, we add a special acknowledgment to the following writers for their contribution to this volume:

Ed Adams
Miner Brotherton
Ron Dwelle
Cathy Dwyer
Bob Gehrman
Jim Gilbert
Scott Henry
Greg Koveal
Nick Nicholson
John Pazereskis
Rick Proctor
Matt Schultz
Jeff Spranger
Sue Weller

# Contents

# Introduction

Commissioning a new boat, whether it is newly built, or just new to the owner, easily rates among the most satisfying of life's experiences; satisfying not only because the new boat represents the fruit of what for most of us is a lifetime of labor, but particularly satisfying because commissioning the new boat provides the opportunity to take an "ideal" boat and turn it into the "perfect" one.

Volume II, *Commissioning and Decommissioning* is divided into two parts. In Part One, "Commissioning a New Boat," we have concentrated on the installation (or upgrading) of the permanent systems aboard the racing or cruising auxiliary. Our goal in commissioning the perfect vessel has been both singular and simple: to provide ship's systems that perform on demand, with the maximum degree of reliability, and the minimum amount of maintenance and repairs. Whether these individual tasks of commissioning are performed by the owner, or by the builder or dealer, the owner always benefits from a thorough background knowledge of each of these systems.

Decommissioning and recommissioning the existing vessel provides the yearly opportunity to renew and rejuvenate the boat, and even to re-experience the joys of commissioning the new boat. What we will refer to as "Seasonal Commissioning and Decommissioning," Part Two of this volume, is the process by which the boat sheds her work-worn surface layers in order to emerge in the spring with a restored appearance and a renewed aura of purposefulness.

In turning *your* ideal boat into the perfect one, we trust that you will find helpful ideas and practical solutions in *Commissioning and Decommissioning*, and in the pages of *The Practical Sailor* and *Better Boat*, from which most of this material was edited.

Keith Lawrence

# Volume II • Part One:
# Commissioning A New Boat

# 1

# A Comfortable Cabin and a Great Galley

## ADMITTING NATURAL LIGHT

The expression "light and airy" is frequently used to describe the ideal cabin interior. Whether the effect is psychological or physiological is unimportant; few sailors would argue that both natural light and good ventilation are requirements of the comfortable cabin. One might assume that the need for lighting and ventilation would be carefully considered by the builder, but beyond the minimum requirements, these needs are usually met with "optional items"; or left to the owner at commissioning time. With a little thought and a minimum of cost, the boatowner can increase his boat's livability in ways that are subtle, but which add up to a big impact.

Light belowdecks can be divided into two categories: natural light, available during daylight hours, and artificial light, available anytime. How you mix and utilize the two types of light can not only make your boat more comfortable, but can greatly ease the demand on your electrical system.

Daylight gets below through hatches, ports, windows, and deadlights. A deadlight is any one of several types of non-opening transparent or translucent devices installed in the hull or deck to let light below. Deadlights include deck prisms and non-opening ports, and can be as simple as a piece of transparent acrylic plastic screwed over a small opening cut in a hatch cover or in the deck.

The key to the successful use of natural light lies not just in the amount of light, but where it falls. You can have blinding light in the main cabin while the inside of lockers or engine compartments are still as dark as the depths of a cave.

## Deadlights

The deck hatch is still a primary source of natural light below. In older wood or fiberglass boats with solid wooden hatches, you can let a surprising amount of light below by simply installing a framed round deadlight in the center of a hatch. Unless the hatch top has a pronounced camber, a 6-inch deadlight will lie flat enough in the top so that bedding compound will make up the slight gaps left under the edges of the deadlight. A smaller 4-inch deadlight will lie flat on almost any hatch, and will let in plenty of light.

Round deadlights framed in bronze, aluminum, and plastic are made by a number of companies and the cost is minimal. Be sure to keep deadlights consistent with the character of the boat; plastic deadlights would look out of place on a meticulously restored classic, and bronze deadlights would look equally absurd on a modern cruiser which already has plastic ports.

## Deadlight Installation

Circular deadlights are easy to install, although the hardest part is usually cutting the hole in the deck or hatch. If you don't mind spending the money, you can buy hole saws up to six inches in diameter which will fit in a heavy-duty drill with a 1/2-inch chuck. Alternatively, you can use an adjustable fly cutter, which consists of an arm with a movable cutter attached to a pilot bit. Because this tool uses a single cutter, it is hard to control when held in a drill motor; it is safest to use it in a drill press, if possible.

The other alternative is to use an electric jigsaw (saber saw). This works fine, although the small diameter of the hole you will cut is a bit of a challenge with this tool. If you are cutting through fiberglass, use blades specifically designed for cutting composite laminates; if cutting wood, use a relatively fine-toothed blade designed for finish cuts in wood. If you're cutting a hole in a varnished wooden hatch top, use masking tape on both the top and bottom of the hatch to cover the line you're cutting. The tape will reduce the chance of splintering the grain around the edge of the hole, and prevents the footplate of the saw from marring the finish. Take your time, use new saw blades, and never force the tool.

Irregularities in a cut made with a saber saw can be sanded smooth with sandpaper wrapped around a cylindrical object slightly smaller in diameter than the opening being finished. A piece of a heavy cardboard mailing tube makes an excellent form for smoothing the edges of a circular cutout in either wood or glass, and lets your enlarge the hole slightly if you need to adjust it to fit the deadlight.

Deadlights can simply be bedded and screwed to a deck that is thicker than about 3/4-inch, but should be through-bolted to thinner decks. If you have a fiberglass deck that is cored with balsa, plywood, or foam, seal the inside edges of the cutout thoroughly with epoxy resin before installing the deadlight. In wooden decks, paint or varnish the inside of the cutout. Condensation will form on metal frames in colder climates, and will discolor or rot unsealed wood.

The bedding compound used will vary with the material of the deadlight frame. Silicone should be used with plastic frames unless the manufacturer specifies otherwise. You can use polysulfide or polyurethane with bronze frames, although we'd be reluctant to use polyurethane because removal of the light would be next to impossible if it were required, for instance if the glass were broken. Because some polysulfides can etch anodized aluminum finishes, we'd rather use silicone for aluminum.

Whatever compound you use, screw the deadlight down firmly and evenly, but not so tightly that all the bedding compound is squeezed out. Deadlights are notorious for developing leaks, but most leaks are the result of faulty installation.

## Homemade Deadlights

You can make your own deadlights out of sheet acrylic or polycarbonate. Don't use any material less than 1/4-inch thick (3/8-inch is better) and keep the deadlights small, since material this thin would not support your weight if you stood on it.

The easiest way to install a homemade deadlight is to cut the deadlight about 1-1/2 inches larger than the hole in the deck, and simply let it overlap the opening. To keep it from being a toe-basher, run a router with a round-over bit around the edges of the deadlight before screwing it down. Even so, the deadlight will stand up proud enough of the surface to be a slight obstacle. In decks thicker than an inch, an acrylic deadlight can be recessed flush with the surface. This requires cutting a rabbet around the edge of the hole to the thickness of the plastic. Because it is mounted flush with the deck, it is not necessary to round-over the edges of the plastic deadlight before installing it.

An oblong deadlight about two inches by four inches, for example, will illuminate a hanging locker, and uses less than a dollar in materials. In addition to being inexpensive, the other advantage of homemade deadlights is that they can be made any shape or size you want. The disadvantages are that they scratch more easily than glass lights, and they take more time to make and install.

## Hatch Covers

Sheet acrylic may also be used to replace the entire top of a wooden hatch, literally making a difference of night and day below. Sheet acrylic 3/8-inch thick (the minimum thickness for a small hatch cover) will bend to any camber you are likely to find in a hatch top. For boats which sail offshore, 1/2-inch thick material is more desirable, and is much less likely to crack if you stand on it.

As with acrylic deadlights, the edges of acrylic hatch covers should be rounded over with a router for neatness. In addition, drilling and installing the fastenings requires care to keep from cracking the acrylic. Holes must be drilled about 1/64-inch larger in diameter than the fastenings used to allow for the expansion of the acrylic as it heats in sunlight.

Acrylic or polycarbonate (Lexan) hatch covers don't last forever. They eventually scratch and craze. Replacement is no more difficult than the original installation, however.

## Deck Prisms

An elegant solution to getting natural light into hard-to-illuminate places is the deck prism. The deck prism consists of a cast glass prism in a metal frame, mounted flush with the deck. The prism refracts light coming below, admitting much more light than you would expect from the size of the hole cut in the deck.

Another advantage of deck prisms is that you can't see through them, making them suitable for mounting over a head, berth, or navigation station crammed with expensive goodies.

A deck prism factory-bedded in a metal frame requires only cutting a rectangular hole in the deck, then bedding and fastening in place. The only disadvantage of the prism is cost. A deck prism is likely to cost about as much as an opening port of a similar material.

Deck prisms are an effective and traditional solution to getting natural light below, and are at home on anything from a traditional, gaff-rigged wooden cutter to a state-of-the-art aluminum IOR boat. In fact, on the modern flush-decked IOR boat, they may be the only way for natural light to get below other than the companionway and foredeck hatches.

Whether you use homemade deadlights or readymade deck prisms, they can be used to light up any dark corner in your boat. They are particularly useful over engines installed under the cockpit, over hanging lockers, quarterberths, and forepeaks. They lighten and brighten your boat, and can make it seem larger and more comfortable.

## Portlights

Another obvious way to get light below is through deckhouse windows or portlights. As a rule, we would be reluctant to change the configuration of deckhouse windows in a production sailboat, unless they are really inadequate, and unless you can find ports completely in character with the ones already installed. One of the most distracting modifications we've ever seen on a boat was done by a well-meaning owner who replaced his fixed ports with larger bronze opening ports. A simple modification like this could knock hundreds or even thousands of dollars off the value of the boat if done improperly. Ironically, even a job well done probably won't materially increase the value of the boat—except to the current owner.

## Extra Hatches

If you want to get really large quantities of light below, the solution may be to add another hatch, or replace an existing deck hatch with a larger one.

Many older fiberglass boats are equipped with fiberglass hatch covers. When they were new, fiberglass covers were touted as superior to wooden ones—no swelling and shrinking, no varnishing, no leaking. After a few years, however, a fiberglass hatch may be little better than an old wooden hatch. Fiberglass hatch covers were usually made with an unpigmented gelcoat on top to let light through, and they do an adequate job of that. But you can't see out of them, and they are usually so flexible that great care is required in dogging them down to keep from distorting them, causing the very leaks they were designed to eliminate.

If you're lucky, you may find a modern aluminum-framed hatch with a clear or smoked plastic top that will fit the existing opening in the deck, not leak, and let you see out as well as let light in.

Aluminum-framed deck hatches are available in every configuration under the sun, although sizes have become somewhat standardized by manufacturers as they compete with each other for the OEM market, which uses thousands of hatches yearly.

Most aluminum hatches are built with flat-bottom frames, and thus fit best on a nearly flat deck. This makes them unsuitable for mounting atop a cambered deckhouse without building a wooden mounting coaming for the hatch—a fairly straightforward carpentry project. Bomar makes one aluminum hatch with a slightly cambered frame to fit a crown of about 1/4-inch in 20 inches, which is enough for the camber of most decks, but not enough for the top of most deckhouses.

Mounting any hatch atop a coaming a few inches high is a good idea. Hatches mounted flush with the deck will usually let water below any time solid water comes aboard, while a coaming three inches high will allow water to swirl past the hatch.

\*   \*   \*

Natural light has many advantages. It is free (after the original installation is made), and natural light is more attractive, since it is the light we are most used to. Natural light doesn't alter colors, it makes no demands on your batteries, and it requires no wiring.

Getting more natural illumination below can be as cheap or expensive as you wish—everything from new hatches costing hundreds of dollars to homemade acrylic deadlights for little more than pocket change. It's a project that requires imagination and a little skill, but it's one of those challenges that makes commissioning a new boat fun. People may not realize why your boat feels bigger or brighter than another seemingly identical boat, but they'll know that it does. And you'll be the one to reap the benefits of a more livable boat.

# BELOWDECKS VENTILATION

Fresh air and dry berths are two rare commodities in the below-decks cavern of most boats. On deck you may be surrounded by endless quantities of fresh air. Below, fresh air frequently comes mingled with similar quantities of fresh or salt water, sometimes in the form of an emulsion that is difficult to breathe at best.

Most boats are well ventilated at the dock or at anchor, or even underway in fair weather. But let the wind blow, the spray fly, and the rain fall, and the interior can quickly become a dank swamp if you leave an opening for ventilation, or an airless dungeon if you don't.

Fortunately, ventilation can be improved almost as easily as natural lighting. In the grand scheme of things, improving ventilation is relatively inexpensive; far less expensive, for example, than installing refrigeration or a sophisticated propane system. And like these other conveniences, improved ventilation will pay big dividends in the battle for more civilized time on the water.

Ventilation can be provided by ports, hatches, variations on the cowl vent, and patent ventilators. Almost all of these can be used either as an extractor, providing an outlet to allow a draft to move through the boat, or as an inlet to force more air into the boat. The combination you use will depend on the deck layout, interior layout, and the way the boat is used.

The ventilation will be different when your boat is under way than when at rest. With rare exceptions, there is no insurmountable barrier to having ventilation that is nearly as effective when a boat is rail down going to weather in a driving rain as it is when at anchor.

## Opening Ports

Opening ports can admit a lot of air below, but they are more useful when the boat is at anchor than when underway. In many production boats, opening ports in place of fixed ports are an option. They are well worth considering. Even if your boat was built without opening ports, it is possible to replace existing fixed ports without too much difficulty.

The variety of opening ports is almost endless. They are available in almost any shape—round, rectangular, oval, and elliptical. You have a similar choice of materials—plastic, aluminum, bronze, and even stainless steel.

When replacing fixed ports with opening ports, be consistent with the other hardware on the boat. Don't for example, install bronze-framed opening ports on a boat with plastic fixed ports and aluminum deck hardware; they'll stick out like a sore thumb. Likewise, you must be very conscious of the shape of the ports. If at all possible, replace existing fixed ports with opening ports of the same shape and size. It will not always be possible to find drop-in replacements, but you can get surprisingly close.

Some boatowners are afraid to replace fixed ports with opening ports for fear of causing leaks. This is a valid concern. An opening port can leak around the outside of the port, or between the frame and the opening. The gaskets in opening ports must be replaceable: they don't last forever. The port should also dog down cleanly, with no distortion of the frame. Distortion can be a problem if you insist on dogging down one side of a port all the way before tightening down the other side (on ports with multiple dogs). Sooner or later you'll bend the frame, crack it, or distort the gasket so that it will no longer seal properly. When the gasket gets old and the port starts to leak, replace the gasket rather than attempting to dog the port tighter.

Bedding the port properly in the boat is also important. So-called "synthetic rubber" sealants vary a lot in their properties. Likewise, oil-based compounds will dry out eventually, requiring removal of the port for rebedding.

Match the sealant to the job. Polysulfides are good for bronze ports, but some experts say they should not be used with aluminum or plastic. Silicone sealants are not incompatible with aluminum or plastic, but since paint and varnish will not adhere to it, silicone should be used with caution to seal ports in a varnished or painted cabin trunk.

Silicone/acrylic sealants are superior to their old-fashioned, oil-based counterparts, and make good general-purpose bedding compounds for ports. Polyurethanes are excellent sealants, but their tenacity is such that a port bedded with polyurethane will be extremely difficult to remove in the future. In addition, polyurethanes may be attacked by teak cleaners, so they should not be used on teak decks or deckhouses.

Opening ports are most effective in two locations on most boats: at the forward end of the cabin trunk, and at its after end. They are also very good for ventilating quarter berths when mounted in the sides of the cockpit well. They will be least effective in the side of the cabin, but will still help.

Underway, the only ports that can safely be left open are those mounted in the cockpit well to ventilate the quarterberths. Under reasonably calm conditions, they can be left open on the leeward side of the cabin trunk, but a single wave out of sequence could ruin your whole day.

## Hatches

Without a doubt, one of the great modern inventions for the boatowner is the aluminum-framed hatch. You can argue about their aesthetics all you want, but they work.

A wood-framed hatch may look good, but it is difficult to make one that doesn't leak. In addition, hatch covers take a fair amount of wear and tear, and if varnished, will have to be tended to at frequent intervals. While a good craftsman can make a wooden hatch that will be beautiful and last forever, the cost of such a job is likely to be high enough to give most boatowners second thoughts.

While heavy, cast-frame hatches are best for offshore use, lightweight cast or extruded hatches are also available, and cost somewhat less. Because of the different uses to which boats are put, it is impossible to generalize about what hatch is best. For most boats, the rugged, more expensive offshore-type hatches are overkill. For a boat used to cross oceans, however, they are almost a necessity.

At least as important as the hatch itself, is the way it is

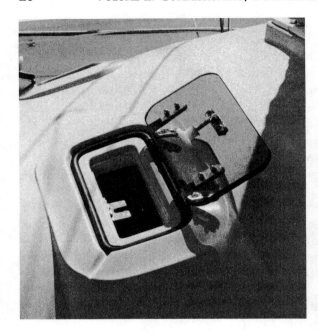

*Small plastic or metal-framed ventilating hatches such as this can provide both natural light and fresh air to small areas such as the head and galley.*

mounted. Hatches are frequently mounted over the center of the main cabin. This is an excellent location both in terms of light and ventilation. But a great deal of the effectiveness of the hatch as a ventilator will be lost if you choose a hatch whose top cannot be reversed to face forward or aft as the circumstances require. At anchor, a partially open forward-facing hatch acts as a giant cowl ventilator, moving tremendous amounts of air below.

To get a rough idea of the ventilation potential of hatches and cowls, compared to one another, consider that the amount of air that a hatch or cowl vent can force below is proportional to the area of the opening. A 4-inch cowl vent has an area of about 12-1/2 square inches. A 19-inch square hatch has an area of 361 square inches. This doesn't mean that the hatch will force 30 times as much air below as the cowl vent, since the efficiency of the cowl vent is greater. However, if the hatch is equipped with side curtains to help funnel the air below, it will provide a significant amount of ventilation.

All this volume of air has to displace the air already in the boat. A hatch over the main cabin, with the open top facing forward, will be more efficient if there is another hatch opened (such as the main companionway hatch) so that air is drawn out the other hatch. An aft-facing hatch over the forward cabin works equally well as an extractor; however, most hatches over the forward cabin face forward, and rightfully so if the door between the forward cabin and the main cabin is shut.

The answer to this problem is to use a hatch with a reversible top. This will allow you to orient the hatch top properly for the desired effect. Be sure to check just how difficult it is to reverse the hatch cover before buying; if it takes a half-hour to do the job every time, you aren't likely to take advantage of the feature often. In addition, check how difficult it is to remove the hinge pins from the outside of the hatch. You don't want ease of reversal to come at the price of a hatch that provides easy entry into the boat.

For most boats with the typical main cabin/forward cabin arrangement, the combination of a hatch over the main cabin, a hatch over the forward cabin, and a small hatch over the head is hard to beat. Remember, however, that a hatch located on the foredeck, rather than on top of the cabin at its forward end, is far more vulnerable to spray, and probably less efficient in funneling air below because of its lower location.

When sailing, a forward-opening hatch is an invitation to a wet interior. Even on a relatively calm day, there's a good chance that the odd wave will drench the top of the cabin with spray, and that the insidious water will find its way below, usually right into the middle of your berth.

While an aft-facing hatch is less vulnerable to spray, it is not immune. You can greatly increase protection without reducing airflow by equipping the hatch with a dodger: a simple dacron hood that protects the open sides of the hatch.

A dodger over the main companionway, either a full width dodger that protects the cockpit or a small one that just protects the companionway hatch, will allow you to leave this hatch open in most conditions.

## Cowl Vents and Dorade Boxes

The weather can get so bad that all hatches have to be closed and battened down. The conditions at which this point is reached vary dramatically, depending on how well designed, positioned and protected the hatches are on your boat. On a lot of boats, the first drop of water sends you scurrying to shut everything. On others, it seems like it can blow half a gale and rain cats and dogs before water gets in through the openings. With a little planning, you should be able to make some progress from the former situation toward the latter.

When buying a boat, make an effort to be aboard in a rain-storm, not only to see what leaks, but to see how much air you can get into the boat when everything is shut down tight.

One good way to get air below when the hatches must be shut is the cowl vent. But like the forward-facing hatch, the cowl vent will let water below in bad conditions. A better alternative is the dorade vent, which consists of a cowl vent set atop a box on deck. Inside the box is a pipe, offset from the neck of the cowl vent, so that air entering through the cowl travels a maze-like, uphill route before being funneled below. The pipe, which allows the air to get below, projects above the deck level inside the box to keep water from entering the deck opening. Small drain holes at the low point in the side of the ventilator box allow water to escape. These drains must be kept small to minimize the amount of air lost along with the water.

The variations on the dorade box are endless, and all, to some extent, work. Whether it's called a dorade or a water trap, the principle is the same; only the details vary. You can buy ready-made boxes of teak, fiberglass, or molded plastic; with opaque, translucent, or transparent tops; with multiple mounting positions for the cowl; and even with multiple pipes through the deck to feed more than one cabin from the same vent.

Like hatches, the placement as well as the size of cowl vents determines their effectiveness. Remember that cross-sectional area is a major determinant of airflow. A 4-inch diameter cowl vent has almost twice the area of a similar 3-inch vent. The rule of thumb is simple: use as big a vent as you can, given the limits of space and aesthetics. An 8-inch cowl vent on the foredeck of a 30-footer may move a lot of air, but it may also look out of place.

Aesthetics play an important role in mounting, as well as in size. If you buy a ready-made dorade box, chances are that it will be flat on the bottom, as if it were to be mounted on a flat deck.

*This fiberglass dorade box is part of the deck molding on a Hans Christian 33. The large cowl vent should provide a good deal of ventilation below.*

If you mount such a box on top of a cabin with a lot of crown, your cowl vents will stick out at an angle like the antennae of a large insect. Cowl vents should stand perpendicular to the waterline, both athwartships and fore and aft. This may require beveling the box in two planes when mounted atop a cabin with both a strong sheer and a strong camber.

Frequently, the most practical location for dorade boxes is atop the after end of the cabin trunk. If there is a companionway dodger, it may be necessary to move them forward, to retain their effectiveness. Air circulation will be improved if another vent is located forward in the boat. Unlike a hatch, a ventilator can be located on the foredeck without compromising water-tight integrity, but make sure that it won't interfere with sail- or anchor-handling.

One advantage of cowl vents is that they are easily turned to face into or away from the breeze, depending on whether you wish to use them as extractors or intakes. For a boat in a slip, this feature can be important, since the breeze rarely fetches straight down the length of the boat.

Because their area is relatively small, it is usually best to pair dorade boxes if possible, particularly when they must ventilate a large area like the main cabin. Over a forward cabin or head, a single vent will usually do.

The so-called "low profile" cowl vents are less effective than taller vents. As a rule, a cowl that is taller and placed higher on the boat will move noticeably more air than a lower vent.

The positioning of cowl vents and dorade boxes relative to hatches must also be considered. They are more effective when placed side by side than if one is placed in front of the other. The worst possible positioning is to place a cowl vent in front of a hatch, since the dorade box and cowl vent will block air flow to the vent when the hatch is open.

## Patent Ventilators

There are numerous patented ventilators on the market. These are all extractors, designed to remove air from the boat. Despite variations, most work on the Venturi principle, so that airflow over an opening in the vent creates an area of low pressure which draws air out of the boat through the vent. Most are reasonably effective as exhausts, but not dramatically so.

An interesting variation on the theme is the solar-powered exhaust ventilator from Nicro-Fico. This vent incorporates a solar cell in the top of the ventilator, which powers a small exhaust fan housed in the ventilator. In bright sunlight, the manufacturer states that it will exhaust 700 cubic feet per hour, the amount of air in a room 10 feet square with a 7-foot ceiling.

Another interesting Nicro product is an interior air circulating system consisting of a small fan mounted in a circular deck plate. The interior circulator is designed to be mounted in a bulkhead (the side of a hanging locker, for example) to draw air through the space. The fan is powered by a small solar cell mounted on deck, just like the solar ventilator.

There are also a number of variations on the cowl vent which are used for special applications other than the ventilation of living space. Clam shell vents used to ventilate engine spaces, for example, are merely highly simplified cowl vents.

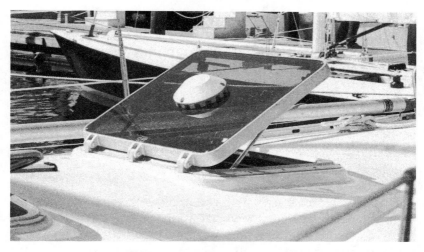

*An aluminum-framed hatch with a patent exhaust ventilator allows air to circulate through the boat even when the hatch cover is closed.*

The varieties of ventilation are seemingly endless and sometimes confusing. But with the careful placement of a few ventilators, it is possible to control the flow of air through the boat quite effectively.

Particularly for those in warm climates, or those who sail offshore, ventilation is an important issue, one which is frequently inadequately dealt with in the original construction of the boat. Fortunately, a little ingenuity on your part can go a long way toward making your boat more livable by improving airflow below.

## MARINE AIR CONDITIONING

While air conditioning might seem an inordinate luxury aboard a sailboat, it is surprisingly practical. Marine air conditioning systems are not inexpensive, but with careful planning, owner-installation is far easier than you might imagine. If you live in a hot climate, and if you have access to high-amperage dockside electricity, air conditioning is worth considering. Since most units are available with a reverse-cycle option at little extra cost, the ability to heat the cabin with the same unit can be an additional benefit to help extend the sailing season.

The most important aspect of an air conditioning installation is the planning stage. Thorough planning is necessary to determine if a unit is practical for your boat. Some of the things you must consider are:

• The location of the compressor unit and the blower fan. Is space available for the unit, and will the space be large enough to allow you to physically complete the installation?

• The selection of a unit with the appropriate BTUs. The BTU capacity necessary for the installation can be determined by using a conversion table and approximating the inside square footage of the area to be cooled. The tables are generally included in the brochures available from the manufacturers of marine air conditioning units. Sailboats are generally easier to cool than powerboats since there is a proportionally lower amount of uninsulated surface area.

• The location of the ductwork and the intake/discharge vents. Cool air must be distributed in a manner that will cool the boat evenly and quickly. Ductwork runs may be physically blocked depending on the construction of your boat. It may be necessary to cut large holes through bulkheads, and you must be sure that this doesn't affect the structural integrity of the hull.

• The location of the seawater pump and seawater intake/ discharge lines. Most 110-volt pumps are not self-priming, and must be mounted below the waterline. This limits the number of locations in your boat where you might mount the pump.

• The location of drains to handle condensation runoff. Every air conditioner produces condensation, and in the humid atmosphere of a boat, the amount is considerable.

• The location of the electrical box containing the control units, and the possible modifications to your existing 110-volt electrical system. An air conditioner will probably draw more current

*A 10,000 BTU reverse-cycle air conditioning unit consisting of compressor, condenser, and blower motor sit atop the settee in which it will be installed.*

than any other item in your boat. Can your electrical system handle the extra demand? (See Figure 3-4 in Chapter 3.)

• The effect of the installation on the overall trim of the boat. An air conditioning system will weigh more than a hundred pounds. This may be an important consideration on a light-displacement boat.

To locate the condenser/compressor unit, it is helpful to make a cardboard mockup using dimensions supplied by the manufacturer. The possible locations for this installation include the inside of hanging lockers, under berths, or in a lazarette. A lazarette is generally the least desirable location being so far aft, since you should try to keep the lengths of the ductwork runs to a minimum to reduce energy loss. The area under settee berths is usually best in most boats since it places the air intake and discharge near the center of the cabin; allows for the simplest installation of electrical wiring, plumbing, and ductwork; and minimizes the encroachment on primary storage space. In addition, this position is very close to the longitudinal center of buoyancy of the boat, so the total effect on trim and pitching moment will be minimal.

## Installation

The first job is usually to fit the compressor unit into the designated space and devise a way to secure it. Securing the unit can be difficult and may require that a mounting platform be fiberglassed in place. In other boats, it may be possible to screw the unit directly to the fiberglass hull liner.

The next step is to run flexible ducts from the blower plenum, an insulated sheet metal distribution box, to the areas to be heated and cooled. In smaller boats, one or two 4-inch or 5-inch insulated ducts in the main cabin, and another into the forward cabin, may be all that is required.

Plumbing must be provided for the raw-water cooling system that makes the unit work. Unlike a domestic window air conditioner, most marine units get their cooling and heating (in the heat-pump mode) capabilities from seawater which is constantly pumped through the condenser unit. If there is an interruption in the water flow, the unit will not function and ultimately may be damaged.

To ensure an uninterrupted water flow, a separate 3/4-inch scoop-type through-hull fitting, fitted with a seacock and an in-line strainer, must be installed well below the waterline. You should resist the temptation to tie the intake water line to existing through-hulls, since an air conditioner water pump needs a great quantity of water.

The 110-volt water pump should be added next, followed by the raw-water discharge line. As mentioned before, the pump usually has to be installed below the waterline, since most are not self-priming. The discharge through-hull should be placed above the waterline, so that when the unit is turned on, you can watch for a stream of water indicating that the water pump is working. If possible, however, keep the discharge close to the water so the noise made by the water discharging isn't annoying to you or to others on boats around you. You need not be concerned about back-siphoning, since the raw-water system is a self-contained, closed system.

Air conditioners produce a lot of condensation, depending

*The large-diameter, flexible duct supplies conditioned air to the plenum box mounted behind each grill.*

on the humidity. The hose used to drain off condensation can be routed under the cabin sole and into the bilge, or into a sump similar to a shower pan that pumps automatically when the water level reaches a certain depth. The trick to draining the condensation is to make sure that the drain lines are gravity-fed. If you don't mind a wet bilge, you can simply run the drain lines straight into the bilge, and ignore the complication of a sump.

With the plumbing in place, the next step is to decide on the location of the thermostat unit, the temperature-sensing capillary tube, and the electrical junction box.

The junction box contains all the relays that are necessary for the unit to operate. It is connected to the compressor by a short wiring harness so that it can be installed in a convenient location. Each electrical component must be tied into either the junction box or the thermostat unit. This means running wiring for the seawater pump, blower fan, and compressor unit. The main wiring harness runs between the thermostat and the junction box, and is usually not supplied with either unit. The harness consists of five wires of varying gauges and color codes, bundled together to form a single cable. Although you can run your own series of wires for this hookup, you can also determine what length is needed, and then order the cable from the manufacturer of the system.

In addition, you have to formulate plans for wiring the unit into the existing 110-volt electrical system, or installing a 110-

*The optional grills range from the inexpensive aluminum household-type to to fancier teak-framed units.*

volt system if you don't have one. You should check the size and condition of existing wiring coming off your shore-power receptacle. If you have an AC distribution panel on your boat, you should also check the condition of the wiring to that panel. An air conditioner draws a lot of power, so each component of the electrical system must be able to handle the required current draw. It wouldn't hurt to check the condition of the wiring on your dock, too.

In the interest of eliminating any wiring problems, make certain that all wiring is protected. Wiring should be sufficiently bundled with tie wraps and hung in areas where moisture can't accumulate. Special care should be taken when installing the thermostat, particularly if the unit is installed in a frequently used locker, since the terminal board behind it carries 110 volts and will deliver a good jolt if you touch it.

The thermostat capillary tube (the sensing device that determines when the unit cycles on and off) is made of soft copper tubing and is somewhat fragile. It is important to mount this sensor in the return air flow to the unit so it can sample the temperature of the air circulating in the boat. Mount this sensor with care since the tubing will kink easily.

In many ways, the most physically difficult job is the installation of the flexible ductwork and the intake/discharge grills. The return-air grill requires no ductwork, since it must be mounted directly in front of the condenser coil. All that is necessary is to carefully measure and cut out the required hole in the front of the locker that houses the condenser unit.

The size of the return-air intake is critical, as it is important to supply the unit with enough incoming air to operate. There are many different sizes of return air grills available from marine air conditioning manufacturers; each has an integral mesh filter which is removable and cleanable.

The discharge grills direct the flow and amount of air, and finish off the visible part of the installation. Various discharge grills are available to fit almost any application, from low-priced plastic units, up to fancy teak-framed models. A plenum or air box is necessary to tie each discharge duct into its grill. Aluminum plenum boxes can be purchased from the unit manufacturer, or you can make your own from 1/2-inch plywood.

The insulated duct can be attached to the boxes with 4-inch and 5-inch PVC couplings purchased from the local hardware store. Other PVC fittings, such as tees and elbows, can also be helpful in running the ductwork.

\*    \*    \*

Careful planning makes the installation of marine air conditioning relatively painless. We recommend that you do it when plenty of time is available, and with the boat out of the water. In the fall or winter months it may be easier to get helpful advice from the manufacturer than during the summer months when they're busy. The installation is fairly complex and the dollar investment substantial, but you don't have to be an engineer to do a competent job. Nevertheless, basic skills in wiring, carpentry, and plumbing are essential.

It's a great feeling to be able to turn on a switch and summon up cold air aboard during the dog days of August, especially when you're stuck at the dock without a breath of air blowing. At that point, air conditioning is almost priceless and makes all the work worthwhile.

# THE GREAT GALLEY

Galleys have come a long way in the last fifty years. Now that sailing is more a family endeavor than a chance for men to get away to be boys, cooking afloat means more than a cold beer and a lukewarm bowl of canned beef stew.

Nowhere is this change more evident than in the galleys of modern production boats. Gas stoves, pressure hot water, refrigeration, adequate storage, and even a modicum of counter space can be realities even in smaller boats. In boats much over thirty feet, these "luxuries" had better be there, or it's no sale.

Before you turn up your nose at such decadence afloat, remember that you wouldn't do without any of these conveniences ashore for very long. So let's be consistent here. A cruising boat, like an army, runs on its stomach. If the person responsible for catering to the sailing body is to do his (or her) job well, then the boatowner must pay close attention to the galley. Cooking is not always fun in the best of conditions; in the worst, it is a trying, tiring experience.

## The Stove

We have a profound prejudice against pressurized alcohol stoves. It typically takes twice as long to boil a quart of water on an alcohol stove than on a gas stove, and every other cooking job is equally prolonged. Priming an alcohol stove is a nuisance, the fuel is expensive and frequently hard to obtain, and alcohol's reputation for safety is, we believe, undeserved. It is about as easy to cook on an alcohol stove as it is on a campfire. If that's your idea of fun, read no further.

In the rest of the sailing world, the American penchant for cooking afloat with alcohol is considered to be as bizarre as our habit of switching knife and fork from hand to hand while eating. Despite some gas stove installations that would make your insurance underwriter's hair stand on end, only a few sailors overseas manage to blow themselves up every year. Far more are injured in drunken collisions between boats than in galley explosions.

If you have a small boat used exclusively for weekending,

chances are good that you have a two-burner, surface-mounted alcohol stove. In most cases, you can directly replace that instrument of inconvenience with a simple two-burner, propane-fired camping stove running off disposable gas bottles.

By screwing the stove to the galley counter and modifying it slightly to provide a means of holding pots in place under the influence of a passing boat's wake, you have a stove installation that is much more efficient than the typical alcohol galley stove.

If you exercise reasonable caution in its use, including storing gas bottles topsides, burning off the gas in the hoses when shutting down, and always watching the stove while it's in use (which you should do no matter what the fuel) there's no reason, in our opinion, that this type of installation is less safe than a "marine" two-burner pressure alcohol stove. It might not be as nice looking, but it will work better.

Large gimballed stoves with ovens take up more space in the galley of small boats than can usually be justified. Unless you're living aboard for long periods of time and addicted to baking, you may find the space required for this type of installation would be better given over to drawers or lockers. A three- or four-burner, surface-mounted gas stove would take up less space than a two-burner stove with oven, and would be more useful for most people.

A gimballed stove is simply unnecessary on boats that rarely undertake overnight passages requiring cooking underway. In port, gimballed stoves should be secured against swinging to avoid accidents, such as the cook being thrown against the stove by a wake and knocking pots over. For most of us, the gimballed stove is more a psychological weapon than a practical one, a statement that your boat is ready to cross oceans at any time.

If you are commissioning a boat equipped with a gimballed range, there are several safety additions you should consider. First, be sure there is a means to secure it from gimballing. The easiest way to do this is a simple barrel bolt installed on the bottom front of the oven. A receiver for the bolt can be mounted on the side of the stove-well.

A safety rail, strongly mounted across the face of the stove-well, can give the cook something to hang onto in rough weather, and can prevent the cook from being thrown against the stove

*Gimballed stoves with ovens take up a lot of space that might otherwise be used for storage in a small galley. Note the guard rail in front of the range to prevent the cook from falling against the stovetop.*

when the boat rolls. Padeyes, securely bolted to the faces of galley counters, should be installed to serve as attachment points for the cook's safety belt.

Gimballed stoves can get top-heavy if several large pots are cooking on top while nothing is in the oven. A top-heavy gimballed stove is extremely dangerous. An action as simple as opening the oven door can dump the whole shebang in the cook's lap.

Sometimes, the gimballing point on a stove is located dangerously low in an attempt to reduce the amount of space required for the stove to gimbal properly. Mounting the stove's pivot point above the level of the top burners means it needs much more space to swing, but it's less likely to end up with a dangerously high center of gravity.

To some extent, you can offset a low gimballing point and

high center of gravity by ballasting the stove with a 10-pound chunk of iron bolted to the bottom. Don't use lead for this, as a hot oven might cause the lead to give off poisonous fumes. The ideal ballast is a thick sheet of stainless steel bolted to the bottom.

Permanent gas stove installations can be made safer with in-line leak detectors. It requires self-discipline to check the leak detector for bubbles, but it's good for your peace of mind.

The remote electronic gas solenoid has become almost universal on boats with permanent gas stove installations, and it's well worth adding if you don't have one. But the solenoid is only as good as you are; it must become second nature to turn the switch on and off every time you use the stove.

Some thought should be given to the positioning of the gas shutoff panel. The ideal location is in the galley, about six feet or so away from the stove. In the event of an emergency, you don't want to have to reach across an inferno to shut off the gas supply.

A panel located in the navigation station with the rest of the electrical switches is easily forgotten. If the shutoff is incorporated into the regular breaker panel, it must be equipped with a status-indicator light which is different from any other lights on the panel. To be of any use in an emergency, the shutoff switch must be clearly marked. The safest solution of all is a panel, mounted in the galley, with a big status light that can't be ignored when leaving the galley.

Another basic improvement to a stove installation that you may want to consider is the addition of removable counter space. This can be either a cutting board mounted atop the stove, or a work surface spanning the entire stove-well in the case of a stove whose top is lower than the top of the well. This larger work surface can be made from a piece of plywood, covered with plastic laminate to match the other galley counters. It can be supported by simple wooden cleats mounted on the sides of the well. If that installation isn't possible, it can simply overlap the well and rest on the counter. When not in use, an underdeck rack can hold it out of the way.

Ideally, the stove-well should be lined with a fire-resistant material such as stainless steel backed with thin insulation board. Almost any sheet metal shop can make up a stove-well liner if you give them a pattern or detailed drawings. The joints

*A gimballed single-burner, bulkhead-mounted butane- or propane-fueled stove is adequate for simpler cooking underway.*

in all stove liners should be welded, not just overlapped, so that liquid or gas fuel cannot migrate out of the well and be trapped behind the liner in the event of a spill. Seamless well-liners are also far easier to clean, with no joints to trap food spills.

For cooking underway on boats without gimballed stoves, a bulkhead-mounted, single-burner swinging stove such as the Seacook will provide adequate cooking facilities.

**LPG VERSUS CNG.** Having noted our dislike for alcohol (and kerosene) and our preference for gas, we should look more closely at two gases commonly used as marine stove fuels in this country. LPG (propane) is the more common, but CNG (compressed natural gas) has been coming into wider use in recent years. Both have advantages and disadvantages.

On the plus side, CNG is lighter than air, so if there is a leak in the system, the gas should not collect in low parts of the boat. For this reason, CNG tanks may be installed belowdecks, without the complicated locker and ventilation requirements of LPG.

Nevertheless, wherever CNG is stored, it should be in a ventilated location, so that any leaking gas can escape. Storing a

CNG tank under a settee or quarterberth which is not ventilated is a poor practice, as gas could be trapped in the locker. CNG burns at about the same temperature as propane, so cooking convenience is comparable.

On the negative side, because CNG is always a gas (propane is a liquid under pressure in its tank) and is not compressed as much as propane, the tanks must be quite large in order to give comparable hours of burner operation. CNG is not as readily available as propane, although the distribution is improving. As long as you sail in an area where CNG is available, that's not a problem. If you want to sail in other parts of the world, it is. Check the availability in your cruising area before choosing.

The cost of a CNG system is comparable to that of a propane system, and the installation, with the exception of tanks, is similar. With a CNG system, you do not purchase the fuel tanks. You lease them, and merely exchange your empty tank for a full one when necessary.

With CNG, your choice of stoves is much more limited than with propane. LPG (propane) stoves are made by dozens of companies throughout the world, as are the tanks and regulators used in propane systems. You can buy propane almost anywhere in the world, and with the proper tank-filling adaptors, getting your American tanks filled in Tahiti won't be a problem. This makes propane an attractive alternative if you plan to cruise to remote places.

## Sinks

Like the gimballed stove, deep double sinks on the boat make her look like a passagemaker. Unfortunately, like the gimballed stove, deep double sinks take up a lot of space. On some boats, the desire for double sinks goes to absurd lengths, with two tiny sinks where a single larger one would be more useful.

Sinks don't have to be big, but they should at least accommodate plates laid down flat or the biggest cooking pot you normally use. Washing dishes on a boat is difficult enough, since you rarely have the luxury of endless streams of hot water to make your plates and glasses sparkling clean. Don't make it worse with a tiny pair of sinks in order to make the galley look like that of a big boat.

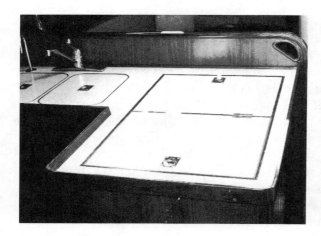

*Drop-in covers for galley sinks, and a flush-fitting icebox lid can greatly increase galley counter space.*

The ideal sink depth is a controversial subject. Small, deep sinks are a pain to use. Large, shallow sinks use water inefficiently if your dishwashing style means a sink full of hot sudsy water. In most cases, a depth of seven or eight inches is adequate, and a sink as shallow as six inches is perfectly serviceable.

There are two advantages to double sinks. First, you can keep dirty dishes in one while washed dishes are transferred to the other. Second, you can stash odds and ends such as bottles of dishwashing liquid, wet sponges, and Thermos bottles in one of the sinks while underway, keeping the other sink free for use.

A Thermos is a simple, valuable addition to any galley. Filled with boiling water before getting underway, it can be used to make instant soups, tea, or coffee throughout the day without firing up the stove. You can either mount it on a bulkhead in a simple wooden bracket, or wedge it into a corner of the sink.

## Water Systems

Few things look classier than a polished brass hand pump in the galley. In many ways, few things are less practical. The advantages of a good hand pump (not a dinky plastic rocker pump that takes five minutes to pump a gallon of water) are simple construction and installation, plus foolproof operation. The trade-off is a certain difficulty in use, particularly in such mundane activities as washing your face.

Foot pumps leave both hands free for washing, but the trade-off is slightly more complex construction, a greater likelihood of leaking, and more vulnerability to damage. In other words, take a rebuilding kit or a spare with you.

Lever-activated foot pumps move more water, but are more obtrusive than recessed foot pumps. In either case, however, mount the foot pump out of the flow of normal galley traffic, where it is least likely to present an obstacle (in a corner, if possible, is best).

Even if you have a pressure water system, it is essential to have at least one manual water pump somewhere in the boat, preferably in the galley. You can always brush your teeth or wash your face in the galley if the pressure water system fails, but it's hard to wash dishes in the head.

If you spend much more than a few days at a stretch on your boat, pressure water and hot water are worth considering. A pressure water system for a small boat can be as simple as a small gravity-feed tank you locate above the water tap. The next step is a small, in-line, single-fixture electric water pump such as the tiny system made by Par. This system can give you pressure water for a total investment of about $30 and a couple of hours of straightforward installation. From there, you can spend as much as you want.

More sophisticated pumps for multi-outlet water systems, including showers, are either diaphragm pumps such as the various Jabsco systems, or impeller pumps like the Paragon. If you're going to have *hot* pressure water, a heavy-duty system is a must.

While the installation of a pressure water system isn't the easiest job you'll do on the boat, it is well within the reach of the average boatowner. For larger systems, you need a dry place to install the pressure pump, a 12-volt power source, new fixtures for the galley and head sinks, and probably some new fresh water piping or tubing. There's nothing mysterious about it, and no special skills are required.

Hot water is one of the great luxuries aboard a boat. You can have it the easy way, with solar-heated water bags or a kettle on the stove; or the complex way, with demand heaters or hot-water storage tanks like small-scale versions of the home water heater.

For a boat that uses gas for cooking, a gas-fired demand hot water heater is the natural installation. While smaller demand heaters can be installed without venting, it's a good policy to plan on putting in an exhaust stack for your water heater, particularly in warmer climates where the extra heat in the cabin would be uncomfortable. The combination of an unvented galley stove and an unvented water heater can put a lot of unhealthy combustion byproducts into the air, which is acceptable if you always have ports and hatches open, but not so good if the boat is buttoned up tight. With a demand heater, no bulky, heavy storage tank for heated water is required, nor is it necessary to be plugged into shore power or to have the engine running to make hot water.

On the other hand, powerboats must have the engine running to be underway, and a water heater equipped with a heat exchanger to extract heat from engine cooling water is an efficient installation. The choice depends largely on the way your boat is used, whether your boat is equipped with gas already, and how much room there is aboard for installing either type of system. The cost is similar with either system.

For living aboard, particularly in colder climates, hot water transcends luxury and crosses over into the realm of necessity. If you sail in parts of the world where the water supply is questionable, or if the water from your tanks has a flavor that makes you gag, a filtration system on the water used for human consumption is a good addition. It does require a separate tap, as it would be wasteful to filter water used for washing dishes.

## Garbage

What can be more of a problem than garbage disposal? In these enlightened times, tossing your junk over the side is unacceptable with the possible exception of long ocean passages, when any other solution may not be possible. A more serious consideration than how to get rid of it, is how to store it until you're ready to get rid of it.

Few boats are equipped with garbage bins, for the simple reason that they take up a lot of cabinet space in an area where space may already be sorely lacking. If you are building or commissioning a new boat and can spare a couple of cubic feet of under-counter space, a pull-out garbage bin is fine. But for most boatowners, the question is where to keep the half-filled garbage bag so it doesn't empty a stinking mess onto the cabin sole. You probably aren't going to be able to hide your garbage— you just want to keep it in one place. An ordinary small kitchen garbage container that can be fitted with a plastic bag is the simplest answer.

A piece of shock cord and a couple of screw-eyes in the side of the companionway ladder or the face of the icebox cabinet will keep the garbage can in place. Rectangular cans are easier to secure than round ones, and stiffer, heavier plastic cans are less likely to be crushed and broken than flimsier ones. A good lid that snaps on securely is a must. A hole drilled through the side of the can and through the lid, with a piece of shock cord keeping the two together will make it even simpler to use.

## Food Storage

Now that you've installed an efficient stove, maximized the use of storage and counter space, and figured out where you're going to keep the garbage, you have one basic question left about your galley: how are you going to stow your consumable stores? With dry foods and canned goods, the choices are limited and the decisions fairly simple; store lightweight dry foods high in the hull, and heavy, canned foods low. But how about foods that need to be kept cold?

Relatively few boats of any size come with truly good ice-boxes. An icebox is one of the most expensive installations on any boat, being intensive in both labor and materials, and taking up a lot of space. People expect iceboxes to perform poorly, and most builders are happy to oblige them.

Before you decide whether to improve your existing icebox, build a new one, or rip it out and install a readymade portable, you should think about how you use your boat, what you really need in the way of keeping things cool, and how much you want to spend.

The traditional icebox, with its cork insulation and stainless steel liner, was a joke. It could eat hundreds of pounds of ice a week, and still manage to spoil half the food. But you don't have to live that way in the age of efficient foam insulation and properly designed boxes. You can even have refrigeration if you want it, but before you spend your money, let's look at the options for keeping things cool.

## Ice

The first option is, basically, to do nothing at all. Use ice. How practical this is depends on how easy ice is to obtain, and how long it will keep in your box. In almost any marina or harbor with a commercial fishing fleet, ice will be available nearby, and it may only require a short dinghy ride to get a big block of ice at a reasonable price.

If a 25-pound block of ice sells for two dollars, and lasts for two days, you can keep food cold on your boat for 100 days a year for only a $100. Of course, you will have lugged 1250 pounds of ice, and spent a fair number of hours rowing or walking to the icehouse. But at that rate, you could afford to haul ice for several years before the cost would surpass that of a typical refrigeration conversion unit.

This is an oversimplification, of course. In places where ice is less accessible or more expensive, you could spend a lot more time and money trying to find it and buy it. On a week-long cruise, it's not unusual for sailors to put into port two or three times, solely for the purpose of replenishing the ice supply. With leisure time at such a premium, this may be a consideration for many boatowners.

Ice has the advantage of cooling a box quickly. You can chip it to use in cold drinks. It makes no demands on your engine, your batteries, and little demand on your pocketbook. But, it can turn into a pool of stinking water in the bilge, if there is no sump, or it can spoil food in the bottom of the icebox, if there is no proper drain.

Ice is also inefficient. It cools by absorbing heat during its transformation from a 32-degree solid to a 32-degree liquid. You're then left with a volume of cold water which will cool things to some degree, but is vastly less efficient than ice itself at the job.

Still, if you use your boat only on weekends, and are prepared to bring both ice and perishables to the boat weekly, ice will do the job at minimal cost.

## Refrigeration Conversion Units

**ENGINE-DRIVEN SYSTEMS.** The traditional option to ice on larger boats is the holding plate system using a compressor driven off the main engine. Holding plates are merely tanks of a liquid that freezes at a temperature lower than the freezing point of water. A compressed refrigerant, passing through tubes in the holding plate, absorbs huge amounts of heat from the liquid in the plate, converting it into a low-temperature ice. As that ice melts, it absorbs heat from the box, cooling the contents. Since the liquid solution is contained in the holding plate, there's no mess in the icebox.

Because the solution in the holding plates melts at a temperature lower than the freezing point of water, it can keep the interior of the box at a lower temperature than is possible with ice. With the proper solution inside, holding plates can also be used to chill a freezer.

There are drawbacks to holding plate systems. They are expensive. A basic system, consisting of holding plate, compressor, condenser, and peripheral hardware, can cost $1500 or more. Installation, assuming you have a good icebox, can double the basic price. Furthermore, you probably won't get more than half your investment back when you sell the boat.

Mounting the compressor on your engine can be a problem, requiring modifications to engine boxes, pulleys, belts, plumbing, wiring, and so forth. Installation of a holding plate system is within the capabilities of a boatowner who's handy and patient, but making it work properly is not an easy job.

Another drawback of the engine-driven holding plate system is its cyclical function. With a good system, it may be necessary to run the engine about an hour a day to freeze the holding plate. Over the next twenty-four hours, the plate slowly thaws, absorbing heat from the box and keeping things cool. Then you must run the compressor again to repeat the cycle.

Even the best systems require daily operation to keep the contents of the box cool. This may be fine if you're out cruising and are running the engine either for propulsion or for battery charging, but it does nothing for you if you're at the office all week and your boat is in the marina or on the mooring. You'll still

*No matter what type of refrigeration you choose, its efficiency will be greatly increased by a properly insulated box with a tight-fitting, gasketed lid.*

have to remove perishables any time the engine can't be run on almost a daily basis.

One way around this is the addition of another compressor driven by 110-volt shore power or the ship's 12-volt power supply. If you're plugged into dockside power, a 110-volt compressor can keep the box functioning all week without attention. Likewise, if you're plugged in and have a battery charger, a 12-volt compressor can do the job while you're away. For this option, you can add about $1000 to the cost of the basic engine-driven holding plate system.

Due to its high cost, a holding plate system is best suited to larger boats, or boats which are used for extended periods. For this type of use, the holding plate system is probably unsurpassed, although you're still tied to the boat when in port if there are perishables aboard; if you're away longer than overnight, you may have a box full of spoiled food.

**HERMETICALLY SEALED COMPRESSOR UNITS.** Somewhere between the icebox and the engine-driven system in cost, complexity, and efficiency, lies the system most familiar to us, because it uses the same technology as your home refrigerator. It is the hermetically sealed, electrically powered, thermostatically controlled compressor/evaporator system.

In your icebox, you install a unit that looks just like the small freezer compartment of an old-fashioned refrigerator. The freezer compartment has room for a few ice trays, but that's about it. The compressor is usually air-cooled like the one in the bottom of your refrigerator. It can be installed almost anywhere in the boat that has a good flow of cooling air.

Installation is simple, involving bolting the evaporator in the box, and joining it to the compressor with copper refrigeration tubing. You then have to get power to the compressor, usually a simple matter of running a couple of wires from the electrical panel. Barring unforeseen difficulties, you can easily install this type of system in a weekend.

There are several advantages. Sealed compressor systems are inexpensive, easy to install, and readily available through mailorder discount stores. The Adler-Barbour Coldmachine, long a popular system of this type, retails for about $800 to $1000 and up, and is commonly discounted by 40% or so. Other systems of this type, such as the Frigomatic and Norcolder, are slightly cheaper.

Since it is thermostatically controlled, the sealed compressor system can maintain a constant temperature in the icebox. Its cycling is not affected by running the engine, as in the holding plate system. You can plug the boat into the dock when you go to work on Monday morning, and have reasonable expectations that the food will still be cold Friday afternoon when you're ready to go again.

There's also one very large disadvantage. The sealed compressor system is power-hungry, and if you lack access to shore power or huge banks of batteries, you could run into trouble.

A sealed compressor system will typically draw from 4.5 to 7.5 amps when running, depending on the size of the system. Have you ever noticed how many hours a day your refrigerator runs at home? Eighteen hours? Twenty hours? With a poorly insulated and sealed box, that hungry little unit could run the same amount of time on your boat. Eighteen hours at 7.5 amps is 135 amp-hours per day. It will take two large twelve-volt batteries to provide this much power when the boat isn't plugged into the dock.

If you have the typical 50-amp alternator with an automatic

voltage regulator, an hour of engine running might at best pump 25 amps into your batteries. At that rate, it would take over five hours of engine running to replace the 135 amps drawn by the refrigeration system. Even with the automatic regulator replaced with a manual one, at least three hours of engine time will be required.

So start out by adding a 75-amp or larger alternator, plus a manual voltage regulator. To that, even for a smaller sealed compressor system drawing only 4.5 amps, add at least another 105-amp-hour battery to whatever you already have on board. Now you've added $400 to the basic cost of the system.

If you're plugged in to shore power and never go anywhere, you can get by with a big battery charger. But if you unplug for more than a weekend at a time, the other additions to your electrical system are a must.

You can, by rebuilding or replacing your existing icebox, greatly reduce the number of hours the system will have to run. But it's still a power-hungry approach to refrigeration, one best suited to dockside living and to powerboats.

You can also increase efficiency with a water-cooled condenser, rather than the normal air-cooled one. These are available as options with some of the systems, but will add $150 or more to the cost of the system. A water-cooled system also complicates installation, requiring a through-hull fitting and a seawater pump.

**SELF-CONTAINED REFRIGERATORS.** For the ultimate in simplicity, you can remove the icebox and install a complete compact refrigerator. These usually utilize the same type of compressor system as units such as the Coldmachine, and have the same power demands. The disadvantages are the same as the other electrically-driven systems. The only advantages are drop-in installation and low cost. Once again, these units are best for dockside living and powerboats, although they're as easy to use as your home refrigerator.

**THERMOELECTRIC MODULES.** It's hard to believe that thermoelectric-module refrigeration units are still on the market. About a decade ago, they were touted as the latest space-age refrigeration technology, offering instant conversion of your icebox to a refrigeration system.

In our opinion, they should have stayed in space. Their only advantages are compactness, ease of installation, and low cost. Thermoelectric modules draw as much power as sealed compressor systems and have no freezing capacity. They will work only in a small, extremely well-insulated box, and even then we don't think they're worth the trouble.

The one exception is the completely portable, self-contained box such as the Koolatron Caddy. You can load it with food at the house, plug it into your car's cigarette lighter while you drive to the boat, then plug it into a similar outlet on your boat. As long as you have adequate power on board, it will do a reasonable job of keeping food cool for a weekend trip. You can then tote it home at the end of your cruise. Portable and inexpensive...but only suited to occasional short-term use.

*     *     *

There are several basic options for cooling food on your boat. Which you choose depends on your sources of power, how you use your boat, the available space for the installation, your handyman capabilities, and how much you are willing to spend.

For a boat kept on a mooring and used only on weekends, it may be hard to beat a few dollars each weekend for fifty pounds of ice. For bluewater cruising, consider the installation work, the cost, and the weight and complication of the batteries and equipment; then decide what it's worth to you for a cold drink.

# 2

# The Plumbing System

## TANKS AND TANKAGE

Tankage is a subject about which there are probably more opinions than there are hard and fast rules. Materials that are generally accepted as suitable for keeping water out of the hull, are often considered unsuitable for keeping it in. The differences of opinion are not limited to various types of metal and plastic tanks in various types of plastic and metal boats; much of the controversy centers around the practice of building tanks integral with the hull.

Industry standards and practices change from year to year. The only universal rule that we can isolate, is the Coast Guard regulation that prohibits integral tanks for gasoline. The designer, of course, can excuse himself from the controversy as fast as he can letter the words "all tanks to be custom fabricated of Monel" across a drawing. But the high cost of custom-built tanks of monel or stainless steel or even aluminum often leaves the owner who wishes to add or replace a tank, in something of a quandary. Let's consider some specifics...

### Gas Tanks

The very word *gasoline* is frightening many boatowners. Just a cupful of gasoline, vaporized in the bilge, has the explosive power of several pounds of dynamite. So while the addition or replacement of a gasoline tank can be a do-it-yourself project, the construction of a gasoline tank is best left to the experts. The reason we say this is, first, for safety and insurance considerations, a gasoline tank should carry a certification plate indicating that it has passed pressure, fire, and vibration tests required by the U.S. Coast Guard and the American Boat and Yacht Council. And secondly, the materials most suitable for gasoline tank construction (Monel, stainless steel, aluminum) are the least suitable for use by the do-it-yourselfer.

FRP (fiberglass reinforced plastic) tanks are in use for gasoline both in marine and industrial applications, and are available in numerous ready-made sizes and shapes. Fiberglass tanks are most often seen installed above deck in open, outboard-powered boats. But as they are frowned upon by insurance companies, and no less expensive than aluminum tanks, there seems to be little to recommend them, other than their resistance to corrosion. It should also be noted that fiberglass gas tanks are not constructed of the same ortho resins commonly used for boat hull construction. Many ultralight monohulls and racing multihulls have gasoline tanks built of epoxy-coated plywood that have been in service for many years. However, most epoxy manufacturers seem reluctant to recommend the practice.

If your commissioning plans call for the addition of a gasoline tank, the first alternative would be to look for a ready-made aluminum, stainless steel, or aluminized steel tank to suit the requirements. If no suitable off-the-shelf tank can be located, the next most economical alternative is to have an aluminum tank custom-built. Since the expertise required for tank construction is not common to all welders, it's best to have tanks built by a shop that specializes in tank construction, rather than the local welding or sheet-metal shop.

One important point to keep in mind with all aluminum tanks is that copper and brass fittings must be electrically isolated from the tank to prevent leaks due to galvanic corrosion. Also remember that fuel tanks need a good connection to ground (not just to the engine block).

## Fuel Oil Tanks
The fact that fuel oil is considerably less volatile than gasoline does not mean that its dangers can be overlooked or taken lightly. But as damage to, or leakage from, a diesel fuel tank is more likely to be inconvenient, rather than disastrous; this fact makes it easier to suggest that an ambitious owner might consider building his own.

Today, fuel tanks are commonly built of aluminum, al-though steel (mild, "black" steel, not galvanized), fiberglass, and epoxy-coated wood tanks are often encountered.

There is little reason (other than cost) to recommend steel for tank construction, unless you are building integral tanks in a new steel hull.

## Water Tanks

Monel and stainless steel are the most often recommended, and most expensive options. There is some evidence that water tanks built of aluminum pose a potential health hazard, although the opinions of medical experts differ. Polyethylene tanks are com-monly used in smaller boats, and seem to last for a long time when they are mounted out of the reach of ultraviolet light from the sun. Inflatable bladders are probably the most common in the larger production boats, and may well be the simplest alterna-tive for adding or replacing a tank in an existing boat.

Fiberglass is ideal for do-it-yourself water tank construction. Cured polyester is non-toxic, and any taste or odor of polyester can be eliminated by adding a box of baking soda per hundred gallons to the first tankful or two. The same treatment, inciden-tally, works with polyethylene and rubberized tanks as well.

## Holding Tanks

The waste tank is the one tank that none of the regulating bodies seem concerned with, at least in regard to construction material. Even those who object most strongly to a stray molecule or two of polyester resin in the water tank, not surprisingly, don't object to a few in the holding tank. There are, however, authorities who care whether or not you have one at all. The basis for their concern, the areas of their jurisdiction, and the zeal with which they enforce their various regulations is a quagmire we leave up to you to sort out.

Several kits are on the market for the retrofitting of holding tanks to existing overboard-discharge marine toilets. Most often, these kits include a small rigid polyethylene or Hypalon-coated fabric tank. The central item in the kit is the Y-valve, which in many cases insures that the "holding" tank never *holds* anything.

The installation of a holding tank in an fiberglass boat, is one instance where the construction of an integral tank may represent the most simple solution. A couple of pieces of epoxy-coated or FRP-covered plywood, glassed into the bottom of a conveniently located locker or into a corner under a berth, can form an acceptable holding tank of whatever size is deemed necessary. Plastic through-hull fittings can be used for hose connections, or short pieces of Schedule 40 PVC pipe can be epoxied into loose fitting holes to form pipe nipples (epoxy adheres quite tenaciously to PVC). An integral holding tank should be fitted with a removable inspection port, so that it can be cleaned out if it becomes clogged with whatever (oh, happy day!).

## FUEL FILTERS

Man has invented few contraptions as reliable as the diesel engine. All it needs is a bit of effort to get it turning, good lubrication and a steady supply of fuel. Unfortunately for diesel owners, that latter requirement is getting harder and harder to obtain. But even if you can't always get clean diesel fuel at the docks, you can be sure your fuel is absolutely clean before it reaches your engine.

Diesel engines, unlike gasoline engines, have very little tolerance for dirt or contaminants, either in their fuel or in their lubricating oil. One reason is that diesel engines are designed with much finer tolerances. Compression in the cylinders is higher, and so is the temperature. Fuel is fed into the engine at higher pressures. Fuel is injected into the engine in precise amounts at the precise time and in a precisely designed spray by injectors and fuel pumps whose internal tolerances are measured in ten-thousandths of an inch. Another difference between gas and diesel engines is that diesel fuel is really a light oil. As it passes through various engine components (including the cylinder head where it also is burned) diesel fuel serves as a lubricant as well as an energy source.

The diesel fuel available at the pump, however, is cruder and less refined than gasoline. It contains dirt particles in suspension, various microorganisms and the worst enemy of all, water.

## The Diesel/Water Time Bomb

Imagine what happens when a tiny globule of water in the diesel fuel approaches the super-hot cylinder head through the injector nozzle. Just when pressure begins to be released as the globule nears the injector tip, the water instantly is turned to steam. The effect is that of a small explosion, that, repeated over time, can blast away microscopic bits from the injector tip's needle valve, which must seat perfectly to deliver the right amount of fuel to the cylinder at the right time for it to fire perfectly.

That's not the only negative effect water has on a diesel engine. Steam and water wash other lubricants away from vital engine surfaces, leaving them vulnerable to rust and corrosion. And, water also provides the necessary medium in which diesel-fuel-eating microbes and algae grow, organisms that in their own right are devastating to an engine's performance and longevity. Even worse, water can also join up with the sulfur present in all No. 2 diesel fuel (sulfur content is about 0.5 percent) to form sulfuric acid, which can have catastrophic consequences, especially in older diesel engines, which allow more fuel and gases to slip into the crankcase from the cylinder head area.

How big a problem is diesel fuel contamination? Diesel engine mechanics estimate that about half of the repair work they do is caused by fuel contamination problems.

## After-Market Protection

Most diesels come from the factory with one or two fuel filters. One is always a cartridge-type filter with a paper element that is replaced periodically. One or both of the filters will also have a valve at the bottom of the filter housing where trapped water can be drained.

These filters are adequate for removing most suspended solid particles from the fuel, but don't do an adequate job of removing water from the fuel. One of the problems with original equipment filters is they don't let you see what is happening. Filters that don't show you if water is in your fuel are particularly problematic, because over time, water will disintegrate paper filters, adding yet another contaminant to the system.

To effectively remove water from the fuel, you need to install a secondary filtering system. The best filters employ centrifugal

*In centrifugal-type fuel filters, fuel is drawn into the system in the middle of the filter, where a spinning turbine forces the fuel into the clear bowl area. Water coalesces around the sides of the bowl and falls to the bottom. Note the water that has collected in this filter bowl.*

action to physically separate the water from the diesel fuel. As an added bonus, these filters also add yet another paper filter medium for removing solid particles.

Here's how a centrifugal fuel filter works: Fuel enters the device and enters a spinning turbine (spun by fuel-line pressure), which spits the fuel against the plastic walls of the filter bowl. Water and other heavier-than-fuel contaminants coagulate and are collected at the bottom of the filter bowl. One of the best things about these centrifugal filters is that you can actually see the water (and some of the dirt) as it collects. They also can be fitted with electrical sensors that short out and activate an alarm when they are covered by water in the bowl (diesel fuel does not conduct electricity). The fuel, now stripped of its water, continues to rise through the paper elements in the filter, and then out toward the engine. Regular water-separator-type filters force the fuel through the filter medium at the top of the filter assembly. Fuel collects, usually in the center part of the filter, as it waits to flow through the filter element. During this period, and as the fuel flows through the element, heavier particles drop to the bottom, where they are drained into a sump or holding area before they are removed.

Of the two types of filters, the centrifugal designs get the nod from the best hands in the marine business. Two non-centrifugal filters will do a perfectly adequate job on most engines, especially engines that are run just several dozen hours each boating season. Still, the best solution is to install the largest centrifugal filter the fuel system will accommodate.

### Filter Installation

You can install a centrifugal-type filter in an hour or two with some careful planning. Most of the after-market filters are designed to be installed on the vacuum side of the fuel lift pump (pressures on the other side of the pump would probably blow the filter apart). If the pump will be above the fuel tank level, you don't have to install a cut-off valve between the pump and the tank. If the tank is higher than the filter, now is the time to add the valve. It's not required by Coast Guard regulations unless you're operating as a commercial passenger-carrying vessel, but it's a good idea to have this cut-off in any case. If the tank is higher than the filter, you need the valve to prevent the fuel from draining into the bilge when you service the filter and bowl.

The best location for the filter is on a bulkhead or some other wood (motion-absorbent) structure close to the engine and the fuel distribution system. Mount it right next to another filter, if there is one already in place. By all means, retain any existing filters (although it's helpful if they all use the same replacement cartridges). Next, decide the right size fuel line you'll need. Most filters have barbed nipples for the inflow and outflow fittings, which accepted both 1/4-inch and 3/8-inch (internal diameter) hose. Use only good, reinforced fuel hose. And use two stainless steel clamps around the hose at every fitting.

For threaded connections, use Teflon tape rather than joint compound. Make sure all connections are tight, but don't overtighten the threaded joints. The housings on centrifugal pumps are usually aluminum and will crack easily. Also, the threads are easily crossed and damaged, so take care when screwing in the fuel line fittings.

## A Helpful Gauge

It's easy enough to glance at the filter bowl after taking on a new load of diesel fuel, to see if water has collected that must be drained. Generally, for most boatowners, filter cartridges need only be changed once a season. The clear bowl makes the automatic warning alarm described earlier somewhat of an unnecessary luxury, especially if you can mount the filter unit in an easily visible and serviceable location.

A less expensive addition to the filtering system, and one that may prove more useful, is a vacuum gauge in the fuel line. This gauge can tell you when your filters are dirty by showing how hard your lift pump is working to force the diesel fuel through the filter system. As the filter gets clogged, the pump has to work harder, increasing the vacuum in the line, which is shown on the gauge. Racor makes a gauge that is calibrated to the breaking strength of the paper element in the filter.

A fuel-line vacuum gauge is a particularly good investment for boats operating in warmer climates, where microbe contamination of diesel fuel is much more common. The microbes are large enough to be trapped by the filter, but don't weigh enough to show up in the filter bowl. One badly contaminated load of fuel can completely clog a filter. The problem won't show up (without a vacuum gauge) until the fuel flow shuts down, killing the engine. This, of course, is likely to happen at a most inopportune moment.

## Fuel Additives

Experts tell us that the problem with fuel contamination is getting worse all the time. Most of the trouble is blamed on sloppy handling of the fuel by distributors and retailers. Diesel fuel seems to have an affinity for water, regardless, and the marine environment presents plenty of opportunities for water contamination. Tank vents draw in moist air as the tank level drops, and rapid changes in tank temperature, caused when sunlight heats up hulls sitting in cooler water, allows condensation to form on the tank walls. One solution is to keep your fuel tank topped off at all times. Another is to use water-absorbing additives, which are available at any fuel dock.

The problem of microbe contamination is a bit trickier. Biocide additives are available to kill off the microbes and the algae. However, they can have two nasty side effects. The first is that when you kill off the little critters, your fuel system is flooded by their dead bodies, which can easily overwhelm the filtering system. The second is that the biocides themselves lower the performance of the engine. We do not recommend adding biocides on a regular basis; use them only when necessary; and then be ready with extra filters to keep ahead of the slimy mass that will attempt to clog the filters and shut down the fuel delivery system.

### Day Tanks
On larger yachts, the best way to prevent fuel contamination is to install a day tank, a smaller tank separate from the main fuel tank. A lift pump fills the day tank only as fuel is required. This tank is not subject to condensation problems and can leave much of the water and slime behind in the main fuel tank.

A point of interest, which illustrates how important it is to keep your fuel clean, is the preventive maintenance extremes to which the U.S. Navy goes on its vessels. Even when its engines are not in use, a Navy ship continues to circulate its fuel through a filtering system.

### Filtering Gasoline Engines
As mentioned previously, gasoline engines are more tolerant of dirt in their fuel. That doesn't mean that they, too, won't run better and longer with better filtering systems. Gasoline (also alcohol, methanol and ethanol) will destroy the plastic bowls used on marine diesel filters. Glass bowls, however, can be exchanged for the plastic bowls.

*    *    *

The total expense for adding a non-centrifugal fuel filter and a vacuum gauge can be less than a hundred dollars with some careful purchasing. With a centrifugal-type filter, the installation might cost half again more. It will probably take you longer to buy the parts than it will to install them.

Considering that clean fuel is the most important gift you can give the most expensive piece of gear on your boat—it seems a small price to pay. What may be the greater benefit is the added independence a good fuel filtering system gives you from the constraints and deceits of land. You will, of course, have to put your own price on that.

# TANK VENTS

For some inexplicable reason, boatbuilders are fond of putting the vents for fuel and water tanks in the topsides on the outside of the hull, usually just below the gunwale. This may be fine in a powerboat, which is expected to stay fairly close to the upright position all the time. It's a simple fact, however, that sailboats heel over when they are sailed. No matter how stiff the boat, sooner or later the lee rail is going under water, and tank vents in the topsides are going with it.

## Water Tank Vents

No matter where a tank vent is located on the outside of a boat, there is always the possibility of contaminating the contents of the tank. The answer for water tanks is to get rid of the external vents. Instead, vent water tanks to the inside of the hull, preferably in a location where any overflow can go straight into the bilge without making a mess of the interior.

Most people object to inside venting for fear of filling the boat up with water after the tank is full. It is true that if the vent outlet is lower than the tank fill, water will come out of the vent before backing out the fill fitting. If you can get the tank vent higher than the fill, that problem is eliminated.

If the water tank is located on the deck, this may mean running the tank vent up the inside of the cabin trunk, which you may be able to do inside the head or inside a locker, where it's unobtrusive. If the tank fill is located in the cockpit sole, the vent can be located under the side decks, under the bridgedeck, or perhaps on the inside of the cockpit well in a quarterberth or locker. As long as the vent outlet is higher than the fill, water will back out the fill before spurting out of the vent, and there is no reason for water to get below.

Keep in mind that the vent outlet must be higher than the top of the tank at all reasonable angles of heel. If it's not, you may accidentally drain the water tank through the vent when the boat is over on its side.

If it is not possible to locate the vent higher than the fill pipe, it only means that someone must be below watching for the overflow of water which indicates that the tanks are full. If a section of clear hose is used in the vent line in a location where it can be seen, there is no reason for any overflow at all. The watcher simply shouts for the water to be turned off when water is spotted in the clear section of the vent line.

Suppose, however, that you don't have anyone to keep a lookout for you, and you don't want to run up and down to watch for overflow. A rather nifty gadget called the Signo is available from International Marine Products (30 Kimberly Ave., Springfield, MA 01108). This simple plastic whistle fits in the vent line. As the tank is filled, air is forced through the Signo, giving out a high-pitched sound. When liquid reaches the whistle, the sound stops, indicating that the tank is full. The Signo was designed for fuel tanks, but there is no reason why it can't be used for water tanks as well.

An inside water tank vent is easy to make. A U-shaped gooseneck is formed out of copper tubing and mounted on a bulkhead using copper plumbing clips. The gooseneck can be linked to the vent fitting on the tank with plastic tubing so that you can see when the tank is full. Remember not to run a copper vent line directly to an aluminum tank unless the dissimilar metals are separated by a section of plastic tubing.

## Fuel Tank Vents

Fuel tanks present another problem. They cannot be vented inside the boat, since the fumes would be dangerous. Venting them in the topsides, however, is asking for trouble. The only advantage in venting a fuel tank through the topsides is to keep spilled fuel off the decks—certainly an advantage, but not enough to offset the potential for water getting into the tank through such a vent.

The most protected location for a fuel tank vent is likely to be the cockpit. The risk in venting a fuel tank into the cockpit is that overflow could turn the cockpit into a skating rink, creating a potentially dangerous situation.

A simple but ingenious solution to the fuel tank vent problem has been developed by Paul Skentelbery, a boatbuilder from Plymouth, England. The tank uses a copper tubing vent line, which goes through the deck up into one of the uprights of the stern rail. A drain and vent hole is drilled in the upright near the bottom, well below the end of the copper tubing. Water would have to fill the stanchion in order to get up to the open end of the vent line.

The only problem with this arrangement is that should the stern rail carry away, the vent would be exposed. It presupposes an extremely strong stern rail, which his boats have. In addition, the opening in the deck through which the vent tube passes must be securely sealed. The obvious advantage is that it makes it possible to get the vent very high, so that overflow through it is impossible in anything less than a rollover. This allows the fuel tank fill to be placed on the side deck if desired, so that any spillage while filling can be washed away without getting the cockpit sole slippery.

If the Signo unit is placed in the vent line below the height of the fill pipe, there should be no reason for fuel overflow through the fill pipe while the tank is being filled. It will signal a full tank before fuel backs out the fill pipe. It does not mean that you don't have to pay attention to what you're doing while pumping fuel, but you should do that anyway. Spilled gasoline is a real fire hazard, and spilled diesel is incredibly slippery.

Probably the hardest part of moving tank vents out of the topsides to a more reasonable location is filling the holes where the vents are removed. You'll need to lay a little fiberglass on the inside of the hull to block the opening, fill the holes in the topsides with an epoxy putty, and then touch up the gelcoat or paint to finish the job. If that sounds like too much work, you could leave the unused vent fitting in the topsides, but seal off the fitting with adhesive caulking from inside.

For some boats, this project may be an unnecessary refinement. But if you cruise or race offshore, it's one worth doing. The necessity for untainted water is obvious, particularly on a long passage. And if you've ever spent hours draining water from your fuel system, moving the fuel tank vent to a sheltered location makes a lot of sense.

# WATERLIFT MUFFLERS

Exhaust systems have always been the Achilles' heel of inboard engine installations in sailboats. Traditional copper water-jacketed exhaust systems are heavy, expensive to fabricate, must be designed to fit each engine installation, and are subject to hard-to-detect pinhole leaks that can reduce exhaust cooling efficiency and cause damage to your engine. In addition, most water-jacket systems have no exhaust muffling effect, so that your boat sounds like a tired tractor.

The waterlift exhaust system has all but replaced copper-jacketed systems in both custom and production boats, in much the same way that the diesel engine has replaced the gasoline engine. The modern waterlift system is just about everything the traditional exhaust system is not; lightweight, inexpensive, and flexible in installation.

Unfortunately, tolerances in the design and installation of waterlift systems are small. There are rules that must be followed and common sense precautions that must be taken if a trouble-free exhaust system is to be the result. Failure to follow the rules can be expensive if water backs up into the engine. Whether you are commissioning a new boat, or installing a new engine and exhaust system in an existing one, it pays to be familiar with the system and the guidelines for a proper installation.

The waterlift is simply an enclosed pot with inlet and discharge hoses. Engine cooling water is injected into the exhaust line near the manifold, gradually filling the pot. Exhaust pressure builds in the pot as it is filled with cooling water until the pressure in the pot is sufficient to blow the water and exhaust gases out the discharge port. Since the exhaust gases do not travel straight from the manifold to the outside of the boat, much

*A waterlift is simply a pot, equipped with inlets and outlets, to hold engine cooling water. The outlet pipe extends almost to the bottom of the muffler.*

of the engine exhaust noise is absorbed in the waterlift, resulting in a quieter exhaust. The exhaust of boats with waterlift systems is usually easily recognized by the fact that the cooling water does not spurt out the exhaust in a continuous stream unless the engine is running at high speed. Rather, water is discharged in bursts, much like the flow through a diaphragm bilge pump.

Most sailboat engines are installed below the boat's waterline. This means that special precautions must be taken to prevent seawater from siphoning back into the engine. A typical waterlift installation for an engine mounted below the waterline is shown in **Figure 2-1**. Note that the top of the waterlift pot is located below the exhaust manifold outlet. It is important that the waterlift be below the manifold at all angles of heel and all degrees of pitch. If it is not, cooling water will simply run back into the manifold and into the cylinders through the exhaust valves.

Cooling water is injected into the exhaust line before it reaches the waterlift. The closer this point of injection is to the exhaust manifold, the cooler will be the exhaust line. The uncooled portion of the exhaust line adjacent to the manifold must be metal pipe, as exhaust gases straight off the manifold are quite hot. Exhaust plumbing downstream of the point of water injection can be reinforced rubber steam hose.

The cooling water discharge hose between the manifold and the exhaust line must loop well above the waterline, and should be equipped with an anti-siphon valve. Check the operation of the anti-siphon valve frequently. These are notorious for packing up with salt, which renders them totally ineffective. If the anti-siphon valve seizes in the closed position, it has no ability to break the potential siphon in the exhaust or raw-water intake line that could fill the waterlift, the exhaust line, and the engine with water.

A common mistake in mounting the waterlift is to place it to the side of the engine, far from the boat's centerline. In this configuration, the waterlift may be above the manifold on one tack at extreme angles of heel. If the waterlift is mounted aft of the engine, this is less likely to be a problem.

The waterlift must be firmly attached to the boat. A muffler half full of water has a certain amount of momentum when it's swinging around under the cockpit, trying to wrench its hoses off and flood your boat.

The exhaust line coming out of the waterlift must loop well above the waterline. However, this loop should be no more than about 33 inches above the bottom of the waterlift. To attempt to lift water higher will create excessive back pressure in the exhaust system, reducing engine output.

If the engine is so deep in the boat that a lift of 33 inches does not allow the exhaust to loop at least a foot above the waterline, the waterlift will have to be mounted above the engine, and the installation becomes more complicated. Rather than injecting cooling water immediately aft of the manifold, there must be a dry stack which rises from the manifold to a point at least three inches above the waterline at all angles of heel. The top of this stack loops downward toward the waterlift, cooling water being injected on the downhill side of the loop. The rest of the installation is identical to that of the system with the waterlift mounted below the manifold.

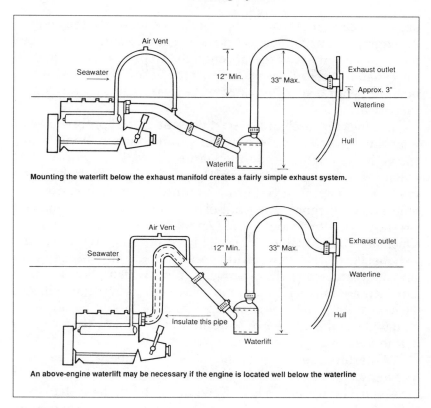

Mounting the waterlift below the exhaust manifold creates a fairly simple exhaust system.

An above-engine waterlift may be necessary if the engine is located well below the waterline

*Figure 2-1*

This dry riser stack is uncooled, and will get hot enough to require insulation. Asbestos is normally used, which should be enough to convince you to try for the simpler muffler installation below the engine, if at all possible.

It is important that the exhaust discharge through the hull be high enough off the water that wave action when the boat is not under power will not create a siphon back into the exhaust system. When the engine is running, there will probably be enough pressure to prevent this, but not at anchor. On more than one boat the engine has filled with water from pitching on the anchor and dipping the exhaust under in heavy weather.

A valve on the exhaust outlet will also remedy the siphoning problem, but it must be accessible, and you must remember to open and close it when you operate and shut down the engine. An engine will usually not start and run if the valve is closed, but if it does start, it may generate enough exhaust pressure to blow the exhaust hoses off the waterlift. If the hose blows off, you will be filling your boat with water and exhaust gases as you motor merrily along.

Engines that are hard to start present special problems with waterlift systems. The raw-water pump starts moving water through the engine while the starter is cranking, but no real exhaust pressure is created until the engine actually starts. If you crank your engine several times without getting it started—a common occurrence with a diesel in cold weather—you may fill up the waterlift without having enough pressure to blow it out. Once again, the water will crawl back into the engine via the exhaust valves. Every waterlift muffler should be equipped with an easily accessible drain valve or plug which allows you to empty the waterlift if the engine fails to start. This drain will also be handy when the time comes to winterize the engine, allowing you to drain the muffler. A waterlift can be split by frozen water left in the pot over the winter.

Waterlifts are made of stainless steel, fiberglass, or even polyethylene plastic. Fiberglass mufflers must be made with fire-retardant resin, as a loss of cooling water in the system from a blocked hose or a broken pump impeller will quickly heat up the exhaust system before the engine shuts down from overheating. The same risk exists with other plastic waterlifts, although they can withstand surprisingly high temperatures.

A cooling water flow detector such as the Aqualarm can detect a blockage in the raw-water system before overheating is a problem. This could prove a valuable asset on a boat equipped with a waterlift system, particularly if the waterlift is of plastic or fiberglass construction.

Waterlift mufflers are a bargain. A plastic waterlift costs about fifty dollars for a unit suitable for a 25-horsepower engine. A good fiberglass muffler costs about twice that, and a stainless steel muffler about the same. Reinforced rubber exhaust hose costs several dollars per foot. The typical small-boat exhaust system, exclusive of the through-hull fitting, should not cost more than $150. A custom-built, copper water-jacketed system, by comparison, would probably cost $300 to $400 or more, provided you can find someone capable of making one.

A waterlift system is particularly practical to use in an older boat when repowered with a different type of engine. It would be pure luck if the manifold outlets of the old and new engines lined up properly, but removing the old water-jacket system and replacing it with a waterlift should be relatively easy.

By following these simple guidelines carefully, you can have a trouble-free exhaust system with very little expenditure of time, money, or effort. This is an anomaly in the wonderful world of sailboat ownership, where the usual rule of thumb is that any task will cost twice as much, and take three times as long as the best estimate you can make.

## THE SEACOCK VERSUS THE GATE VALVE

No matter how strong a hull may be, a hole through that hull will allow water to enter. Let that water enter unimpeded for any length of time and you have a boat that's sitting on the bottom.

The best solution to this frightening prospect is to have no holes. This means no engine cooling-water intake, no intake or discharge for the head, no overboard sink drains, no cockpit drains, no electronic sensors, and no rudder or propeller shaft stuffing boxes. No holes is thus an unreasonable solution. Clearly a number of through-hull openings are needed. The first concern, however, is to reduce the number and size of such holes to a minimum and to have as many as possible penetrate the hull above the waterline.

Those below the waterline must have fittings and connections—hose or pipe—that maintain the integrity of the hull structure. Consider the inherent strength of a cockpit drain consisting of a length of thin-walled plastic hose attached to a fitting with a simple hose clamp. Then consider what can happen when the storm anchor fetches up against that hose because it has slipped down into the bilge when it was lowered into the bottom of the lazarette. Now *that's* scary.

Strong connections and clamps are not enough, however.

Every through-hull fitting needs a rugged and durable valve capable of being quickly, easily, and positively closed; either in the event of the failure of a connection, or merely as a precaution when the boat is left unattended.

It has become a common practice for builders to reduce the cost of their products by playing fast and loose with out-of-sight, out-of-mind fittings as those for through-hull openings. For openings above the waterline (even those that are below the water when the boat is heeled) they attach hoses directly to fittings with no valves. For openings below the waterline, they install a variety of valve devices, most of them fulfilling the rudimentary requirement of shutting off the flow of water; but many of them inadequate to resist electrolysis, accidental blows, or the torque generated when being closed.

Proper marine seacocks attach directly to the hull to take the strain of hoses and piping off the through-hull fitting and transfer that strain to the hull structure. They are fabricated of bronze alloys, stainless steel, and most recently of plastics. They are fitted with a lever handle that indicates at a glance whether they are open or shut.

Seacocks require lubrication either through a nipple or by disassembly. This is vital because the tolerances in a proper seacock are small, and they are prone to seizing without periodic lubrication. A seized seacock is of no value if a hose or pipe connection breaks.

Seacocks, however, are expensive. For a modest-sized craft with a half-dozen through-hulls, the investment for plastic seacocks could easily be more than $200; for bronze seacocks, more than $500. Contrast this figure with the less than $100 for through-hull openings fitted with simple gate valves. Gate valves are the same valves sold at plumbing supply stores for use with hose or pipe. Such valves use a circular handle to turn down a disk or "gate" to close off flow.

It is difficult to tell whether a gate valve is closed. Even with a careful examination, it is difficult to see by looking at the handle whether the gate is fully closed. Likewise, an obstruction lodged under the gate can make the handle feel tight, indicating the valve is closed, but actually leave the valve open.

Worse is the fact that many models of ordinary gate valves

are made of materials (especially brass) that are highly subject to electrolytic or galvanic corrosion. The brass or other alloys containing zinc can, within a disturbingly short time, become "dezinctified" making the metal porous and weak. Despite no outward signs of weakness, the valve can fail without warning.

Beware, however; the fact that a seacock *seems* to be made of metals that are more corrosion-resistant is no guarantee against an early failure. At least one line of boat built in the Orient has a grim reputation among surveyors. Its locally-cast bronze seacocks, patterned after a well-known and dependable U.S.-made seacock, are so subject to electrolysis that they are almost universally noted by surveyors in their reports.

A better choice than the gate valve is the ball valve. These are relatively expensive, but they are made to exacting specifications that call for corrosion-resistance, strength, and close tolerances. The better versions use Teflon or nylon seals that eliminate the need for lubrication. Moreover, they have lever handles so that their status, open or shut, is immediately apparent.

At the very least, all underwater through-hull fittings should have marine valves with lever handles readily accessible even in a bilge full of water. All such fittings above the waterline should also have valves, preferably seacocks, but readily accessible, marine-quality gate or ball valves are acceptable.

Every two seasons every through-hull fitting and valve should be thoroughly examined, lubricated if called for, and rebedded if necessary. Hose clamps (doubled on all underwater connections) and threaded pipe connections should be checked and tightened annually. Hoses and pipes should get the same inspection and be replaced at the first sign of wear, cracking, or corrosion. Incidentally, use only reinforced hose intended for high-pressure applications.

The use of cheap gate valves in a production boat does not necessarily mean that the builder is otherwise scrimping on the quality of his product or on elemental safety. Evidence, yes; proof, no. The low price of the new reinforced nylon marine seacocks make the use of gate valves a highly questionable source of savings. When ordering a new boat, you can insist that the builder install proper fittings to your specifications, deducting the cost of the standard valve from the higher cost of seacocks. When recommissioning an existing boat, consider up-grading gate valves on underwater through-hulls to the safer, more seamanlike seacock.

# DRINKING WATER
# PURIFICATION SYSTEMS

While most U.S. water sources are relatively free from carcino-gens, bacteria, protozoa, and viruses, unfortunately, this is not always the case in undeveloped parts of the world, including some of the islands of the Caribbean.

In talking with a number of people who have cruised in remote areas of the world, we have encountered remarkably few cases of illnesses attributed to contaminated water. Neverthe-less, caution should be exercised when filling water tanks in out-of-the-way places; local people may have no trouble drinking water which will give the visitor a case of the heebie jeebies.

There are a number of different approaches to rendering unknown water safe, or at least safer, for consumption. Among these are filtration, chemical treatment, heat sterilization, distil-lation, and reverse osmosis. Filtration is possibly the most prac-tical method for use aboard a small boat.

Multi-stage filters such as the Seagull IV manufactured by General Ecology, Inc. (P.O. Box 320, Paoli, PA 19301) which can be installed in the fresh water line, will remove asbestos, bacteria and other microorganisms, and any suspended particles down to .4 micrometers in size. Unfortunately, the virus which causes hepatitis is even smaller, and cannot be removed by any filtra-tion system we are aware of specifically designed for installation on a boat.

All filtering systems require periodic replacement of the filter element. The replacement intervals vary with the type of filter, the amount of use the filter has, and the amount of material that must be removed from the water. Since this is unpredictable, you must always carry spare filter elements, which are not likely to be available where you are cruising.

Chemical purification involves treatment with chlorine or iodine. This will kill virus or bacteria, but does nothing to remove particulate matter or asbestos fibers. Water can be chemically treated in the ship's tanks, or individual batches may be treated just prior to use. Halazone is a commonly available water-purification chemical which contains chlorine. The quantities of chlorine required for water purification would not be likely to harm an aluminum water tank, but chlorine is a powerful oxidizing agent and does accelerate corrosion.

The Everpure system, by Everpure (660 N. Blackhawk Drive, Westmont, IL 60559) is a chlorination/dechlorination system which installs between the tanks and your faucet, so that chlorine is not added to the tanks. Everpure also has a filter to remove particulate matter.

Sterilization is another alternative. Like non-filter chemical treatment it does not remove particulate matter, but it is simple, requires no additional equipment, and is reliable. Sterilization is a fancy word for boiling water before using it. This may be a little inconvenient, but it works.

Mimi Dyer, who circumnavigated with her husband Dan in the early 1970s, reports that they knew of cruising people who became ill from contaminated water, although they never had any problems aboard their own boat. The Dyers always added chlorine to their water tanks. Their formula was very simple; they added liquid bleach until they could taste the chlorine. If the taste hadn't dissipated after a few days, they added more water and less bleach the next time. In 40,000 miles of sailing, they never had any trouble with water by using this system.

A sort of cruising grapevine develops among the fraternity of long-distance sailors which tells you where to get clean water, and what water sources to avoid. Since this may change over time, a water source that was reliable a few years ago may no longer be so by the time you get there, so you need to plan alternatives. In addition to some method of filtration or purification, it is always advisable to carry spare jugs for water in case a questionable water supply must be used. The questionable water supply can be kept in jugs rather than risk contamination of the ship's tanks, and can be used for washing, but not for drinking or cooking.

With reasonable precautions and the judicious conservation of good water when you find it, including catching your own in the frequent showers of the tropics, it is possible to cruise with confidence in the safety of your fresh water, that most precious of commodities.

# REVERSE OSMOSIS DESALINATION

Although there is no substitute for safe, fresh water, there is an alternative to filtration systems and chemical additives.

Until recently, only very large powerboats or motorsailers could make their own drinking water from seawater as they needed it. This was usually done by distillation with low-pressure evaporators utilizing waste engine heat. While this is a very effective process that produces absolutely pure water, the units are large, heavy, and expensive.

Today, there is reverse osmosis, and sailing vessels in the 30- to 50-foot range may elect to make their own water instead of hauling the weight of tank water around with them (a gallon of water weighs 8.34 pounds). These devices are known as water-makers or desalinators. Reverse osmosis (RO) has been described as the fastest, most efficient and most economical method of converting seawater to fresh water. Desalinators require less power, less space and equipment, and generate far less heat than other systems. Typical sizes run about four or five cubic feet and most weigh only a hundred pounds or so.

Before describing reverse osmosis, we should briefly review what osmosis is. Osmosis is often described as "diffusion through a semi-permeable membrane." A standard demonstration involves a sugar solution (molasses or syrup in water), water, and cellophane as the membrane that separates the two liquids. The membrane is stretched over the bottom end of a long tube and secured with a rubber band. The sugar solution is poured into the tube, which is then immersed into a beaker of water and the original height of the solution is marked. After a short time it will be noted that the level inside the tube rises as water from the beaker passes through the membrane and enters the solution. Semi-permeable means that the water molecules can pass into the solution, but the sugar cannot go the other way. Eventually, equilibrium is attained and the few inches increase in height of the solution above where it started is called the *osmotic pressure* for the system. The same thing will happen with a seawater solution and water—with astounding results.

In order to *reverse* the process, you have to apply an equivalent pressure to the solution side of the membrane. Then the water molecules will be "squeezed" out of the solution and pushed back through the membrane. That is essentially what happens in a reverse osmosis desalinator. Raw seawater (feed water) is first passed through several filters to remove suspended materials and oil that could clog and damage the sensitive membrane, then a high-pressure pump boosts the pressure up to 800 to 1,000 PSI and delivers the feed water to the spiral-wound membrane located in a high-pressure vessel. As the pressurized seawater passes over the surface of the membrane, some pure water molecules pass through the membrane where they will be collected on the other side as "product water," not quite absolutely pure (most guarantee 98.5 percent minimum salt rejection), but certainly good enough for drinking and in many cases, better than what we get at home. The remaining seawater is pushed from the pressure vessel by incoming water and flushed overboard. Less than 10 percent of the feed water is converted into product water. The fresh water, after passing a salinity test for purity, is pumped off for storage.

So all one really needs is a special membrane, a high pressure pump (electric, engine-driven mechanical, or hand) and some seawater. These are the essential ingredients. Everything else is peripheral, although the system might not work as well or for as long without them.

In researching this chapter, we identified ten different manufacturers of RO desalinators who advertise in the boating press. They produce a wide variety of products, with various water-producing capacities (gallons per hour or gallons per day), and this, of course, mostly determines the initial price of the unit. But also, when larger, higher output systems are available, they invariably use larger pump motors, which require more power to run; now we're talking about motors of several horse-power that require 20 or so amps at 115 volts AC.

If you decide to go this route, realize that most reverse osmosis systems work on AC, and that the watermaker will be the largest user of alternating current aboard. If you don't have sufficient reserve capacity with your present generator, then you must consider the expense of a new generator as well as the cost of the desalinator.

When it comes to pricing out a desalination package for your boat, you may find the list of options baffling. Some manufacturers include as standard equipment such items as three-stage filtration, including an oil separator; others sell the oil separator only as part of an expensive option package. Which is now the better buy? Only you can decide that.

All manufacturers list an ultraviolet sterilizer as optional, and most cost about $500. Do you need one? If you ever plan to operate the unit in sewage-contaminated waterways, you do. While few bacteria get through the membrane into the product water (the amount increases with the age of the membrane), most viruses pass right through it. The ultraviolet sterilizer destroys practically all (99.8 percent) viruses, bacteria and other pathogens in the product water before it goes to storage, thus ensuring a safe drink regardless of the feed water origin.

Other accessories include an alarm to warn of system failure, an installation kit, a spare parts kit, membrane cleaning kits, expansion kits to increase the output capacity, a remote control panel, a charcoal filter and so on. Some models have the membrane pressure vessels exposed or remote from the main unit, others are contained inside the housing.

The entire process of reverse osmosis is temperature sensitive. The rated output is usually specified at a feed-water temperature of 77 degrees F. Productivity increases with higher temperatures and decreases with lower feed-water temperatures; that's why they say output may vary by 15 percent, plus or minus. Temperatures in excess of 110 degrees Fahrenheit can damage the membrane, however. This gives an advantage to the remote or exposed pressure vessels in that the pressure vessel module with membranes inside can be mounted in a cool location while the rest of the unit is in the hot engine room along with the vessel's other machinery. High temperatures and oil are natural enemies of the RO membrane; so are freezing, drying out, and sitting idle.

Count on replacing membranes every 1-1/2 to 2-1/2 years.

The cost of this membrane replacement largely depends on whether the membrane is removable from the pressure vessel or whether the entire assembly must be replaced. They come both ways, so consider this before deciding which model might be best for you. Other routine maintenance will include cleaning or replacing pre-filter elements and replacing the high-pressure pump seals every 1,500 to 2,500 hours of operation. The preventive maintenance kit for these operations will run from a hundred dollars to several hundred dollars.

Not all reverse osmosis desalinators run on AC, but all the higher output units do. Only a few models are available with 12-volt DC motors. One is rated at 90 gallons per day, which is 3.75 gallons per hour, but the unit uses a 1/2-horsepower motor, and spinning it draws an incredible 28 amperes! Look up the wire size required by that kind of current, and you will see that selecting 12-volt DC just because you already have it aboard is not always the best criterion. Chances are your present battery bank and alternator will not be able to supply that kind of load for very long—certainly not on the sustained basis that a watermaker demands.

If it looks like reverse osmosis desalination might be in your future, rather than simply rebuilding your 12-volt DC system to accommodate it, you also should get a price quote on adding an AC generator of sufficient capacity for comparison. See what the added weight will do to your vessel's trim as well. Another 12-volt DC model (Seagold) is so modest by comparison with all the other ones available that we might unwittingly pass it off as a toy. But look it over first. It draws only four amps while producing 1-2/3 gallons per hour. At the recommended duty cycle of 10 hours per day, that's almost 17 gallons per day. Forty amp-hours should be within the available electrical storage capacity of a well-equipped cruising sailboat, and 17 gallons is three or four days' worth of water for a cruising couple. In addition, this model is simple, compact and light in weight. It is the only one that comes with a pump handle for manual operation. But in spite of its multifaceted "smallness," it is not inexpensive, costing almost as much as its bigger cousins.

We know of only one engine-driven desalinator, which produces a little over four gallons per hour. An electromechanical drive transmits power from the engine to the high-pressure pump through a belt-driven magnetic clutch. It will pull two horsepower from your engine, which won't get to the prop while this unit is working. If you have only eight or ten horsepower to start with, that's something to think about. In addition, the feed-water pump and accessories will require a maximum of six amps at 12 volts DC. If your boat is now somewhat overpowered in the engine department, this could be a good choice. It's surely cheaper than adding an AC generator.

Seagold Industries (7672 Winston St., Burnaby, B.C., Canada V5A 2H4) is the only manufacturer of a hand-operated water-maker. They have two models, both sold as life raft survival equipment. One (The Survivor) makes one cup in 13 minutes, and the other produces 1.5 gallons per hour as long as you can keep pumping. Neither appears practical as the only supply of fresh water aboard a cruising sailboat, but certainly they are worth considering in place of solar stills for your emergency "abandon ship" package.

# 3

# The Electrical System

## TWELVE-VOLT SYSTEM BASICS

The lead-acid battery has made possible the use of space-age equipment aboard yachts that was not even dreamed of twenty years ago. Today the electrical system has become one of the most important systems aboard, perhaps second only to propulsion and steering, and often they too are dependent on the electrical system. The venerable lead-acid storage battery holds center position.

The following is a guide for the proper selection, use, and care of your 12-volt batteries, from choosing the correct size to the best method of charging to ensure a long life from your battery investment.

### The Theory

There are two kinds of energy in the world, renewable and non-renewable. Diesel, gasoline, propane, and kerosene are examples of non-renewable energy. Bio-fuels, solar, hydro, wind, and so on are renewable energy sources.

For the sailor, however, virtually everything tangible aboard becomes non-renewable at sea. Electricity is especially interesting to the cruiser because alternative energy sources such as photovoltaics, wind, and water generators, in conjunction with a storage system, mean it can be treated like renewable energy.

Energy storage may be reversible or non-reversible. Non-reversible energy aboard is typically found in a few basic forms. Zinc-carbon batteries, chemical light sticks, and canned Freon for the air horn are examples of non-reversible stored energy. Once the stored energy is released, it's gone.

Reversible storage elements allow us to "capture and conserve" power when it is available and use it later when we want it. Lead-acid batteries are reversible storage elements. A holding plate refrigeration system similarly uses a reversible storage element in the form of a eutectic solution.

Reversible storage can be looked at as a way of wringing out every last ounce of energy possible from the non-reversible energy aboard, such as diesel fuel. Think of this as slowing down entropy, if you will. If the boat is steaming from port to port, or if engine time is required for mechanical refrigeration, then some of the engine's excess power may be converted to electricity and stored for later use.

The cruising boat has to make the most out of every ounce of fuel aboard. When trying to minimize engine time, you want the most efficient and fastest conversion from non-reversible stored energy (diesel fuel) to DC power in batteries or cooling for refrigeration. Ideally, one would store an infinite amount of power in zero running time.

The problem with too many systems is that the reverse seems true—nearly zero power is stored in what seems like infinite running time. Poor design is the culprit.

### The System

Batteries are part of a system which begins with the "load." Refrigeration, starter motors, bilge pumps, fresh-water pumps, lights, electronics, inverters, and microwaves all demand power. The amount of power required depends on the needs and desires of each owner. If you really want a proper system, spend a few minutes and estimate your daily power consumption while cruising.

The best way to find out how much electricity a particular device uses is to read the name-plate data, which usually gives consumption in amps or in watts. If it is given in watts, simply remember that watts is equal to volts time amps. For example, a 60-watt load on a 12-volt system uses 5 amps.

**Figure 3-1** gives approximate loads used by a variety of on-board electrical devices. The table is an estimate of the typical daily consumption aboard a cruising sailboat while cruising. This is actually a very conservative daily power consumption.

## Figure 3-1. Average Power Consumption

| Device | Amps | x | Hours used per Day | = | Amp-Hours per Day |
|---|---|---|---|---|---|
| Bilge Pump | 5.0 | | .25 | | 1.25 |
| Cabin Lights | 2.0 | | 4.0 | | 8.0 |
| VHF receive | .5 | | 4.0 | | 2.0 |
| transmit | 5.0 | | .25 | | 1.25 |
| Tricolor 20W | 1.7 | | 8.0 | | 13.6 |
| Compass Light | .2 | | 8.0 | | 1.6 |
| Depth Sounder | .5 | | 2.0 | | 1.0 |
| Knotmeter | .1 | | 24.0 | | 2.4 |
| Loran | 1.0 | | 4.0 | | 4.0 |
| Autopilot | .5 | | 8.0 | | 4.0 |
| Freshwater pump | 5.0 | | .1 | | .5 |
| Stereo | 1.0 | | 8.0 | | 8.0 |
| | | | **Total Amp-Hours Per Day** | | 47.6 |

Increase the use of the stereo, Loran, autopilot, or add radar, SatNav, marine SSB, or ham radio gear and the power consumption could soar over 75 and head toward 100 amp-hours per day. And we haven't even touched on that most popular of all power-hungry options—refrigeration. If you have DC refrigeration, add 50 amp-hours per day in a cool climate and as much as 100 amp-hours per day if you're cruising in southern waters.

The decisions you make will all affect the electrical system. Your boat should be tailored to your desires. Some folks need ice—life without a cold drink is not part of the cruising life they are interested in. It is true that loads can be shed (you can turn the refrigerator off); the question is, do you want to? If radar, radios, refrigeration, power tools, stereos, and even television are things you want, you can have them, if you plan for them.

In the power system for your boat, there are really only two decisions that drive the entire design, and they are both in your control. The first is, what is the load (how many amp-hours will you consume)? The second is, how long do you want to run it without recharging?

Ideally, we would like a system designed for a minimum of a four days. We think that such a system has the reserve capacity to stand up to heavy loads when needed and the storage necessary for several days of minimal power consumption with absolutely no charging in an emergency.

## Storage

The amount of energy that a system can hold is its storage capacity, a primary variable in total system capacity. A battery's capacity is measured in "amp-hours." For example, if a load uses 5 amps and runs for 12 hours it has used 60 amp-hours. It follows that a battery with a capacity of 60 amp-hours could supply this load. Right?

Wrong. Batteries are a little more complicated. The following tells you how batteries work and how to determine what battery capacity you need for your system. Once you understand how a battery works, then you can choose the right battery with the right capacity and charge it properly.

## Battery Basics

Batteries are black, heavy, ugly, and lurk in dark inaccessible corners; they smell; they eat your blue jeans. The basic chemistry and construction of batteries has been known for over 100 years and isn't that tough to understand. In fact, your old high-school physics book probably has a very clear discussion of electro-chemistry and a diagram, similar to **Figure 3-2**, illustrating the four different states of the battery.

The word *battery* really means a group of cells, each with a nominal voltage of 2 volts. Thus a battery with six cells has a potential of 12 volts. Figure 3-2 shows how each cell behaves.

When the battery is fully charged, the negative plate is composed of a spongy lead paste, and the positive plate is composed of a lead oxide paste. The pastes are held in place with a grid, also made of lead. The grid physically supports the paste and serves as the current conductor. The positive and negative plates are held apart by separators and insulators. These assemblies are immersed in a solution of sulfuric acid and water (known as the electrolyte) with a specific gravity (SG) that defines the concentration.

The fully-charged "at-rest" voltage of the cell is equal to the specific gravity of the electrolyte plus 0.84. In other words, six of these cells, connected in series to make a 12-volt battery, filled with typical electrolyte of 1.2650 specific gravity, will have a fully charged open-circuit voltage of: $(1.265 + .84) \times 6 = 12.63$ V.

When a load is applied, the battery discharges, current flows,

# Figure 3-2. Chemical Reactions Within the Lead-Acid Cell

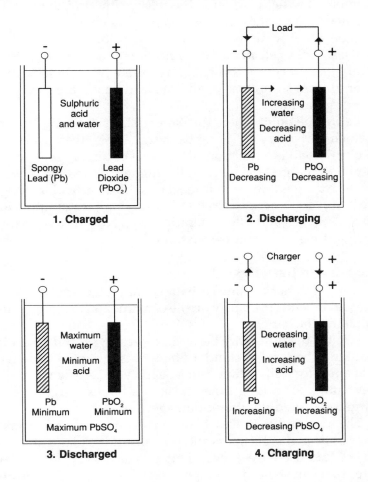

and work is done. The electrochemical reaction driving that work causes the surface of the plate to become converted to lead sulfate and reduces the ratio of sulfuric acid to water. Electrons are given up in the process; they do the work.

To increase the battery's capacity, the plates are made as porous as possible in order to increase the surface area available during the chemical reaction. If a battery is deeply discharged, the plates become covered with lead sulfate crystals with a very tight, dense structure. If they cannot be broken down and recombined with the water in the cell by charging, the battery is "sulfated." This is the reason that batteries should not be allowed to become totally discharged and remain so.

If a source of electricity is connected to the lead-acid storage battery, the process is reversed; the sulfate recombines with the water to form sulfuric acid, and the lead pastes are returned to their original form.

Below the point where the battery starts "gassing," the rate at which the battery will accept a charge and convert lead sulfate to sulfuric acid is a function of the level of discharge. The more deeply discharged the battery, the higher the acceptance rate.

Once the gassing point is reached with a particular charging rate, the excess energy goes into hydrolyzing water into hydrogen and oxygen and into generating heat. No effective charging is being done any longer at that rate.

## Deep-Cycle Batteries

The total number of times a battery may be charged and discharged depends primarily on the construction techniques used in making the battery.

What is the difference between a deep-cycle and a standard "cranking" battery? A standard battery is designed to deliver a lot of amps for a short time, but a deep-cycle battery will deliver a few amps for a long time and it can be discharged and recharged repeatedly without damage.

The major differences between deep-cycle and cranking batteries lie in the thickness and porosity of the plates and in the alloy of lead used. Deep-cycle batteries have very heavy, dense plates that can stand up to repeated cycling. Antimony is often a key component in deep-cycle batteries. Antimony alloyed with lead yields a strong, relatively dense, long-lived plate. Since the battery is required to deliver a lighter load for many hours and then be recharged, this strength and density is a must. The disadvantage of antimony is that after time, some of it migrates to the negative plate and thus "poisons" the battery. This effect is reduced by proper charging.

The life of a deep-cycle battery, properly treated, can be up to 15 or 20 years, but that sort of performance is not what observation shows as the average useful life of most battery installations. Poor maintenance shortens the life of most batteries to 20 percent to 30 percent of what is possible with good care.

Maintenance-free cranking batteries have an overall plate construction that is thinner and less robust than deep-cycle batteries. Additionally the plates are more porous, allowing acid to easily flow through the paste, thus giving a high surge-current capacity. They are often constructed from a lead alloy containing calcium. The calcium helps reduce water consumption.

The calcium alloy has a few disadvantages. The adherence of the active plate material is reduced; thus premature failure due to "mud-shedding" is more likely. Mud-shedding refers to the sloughing off of plate material during the course of a battery's life. The "mud" builds up in the bottom of the cell, eventually shorting the plates, causing total battery failure. Poor charging techniques hasten the shedding process.

Another problem is the formation of high-resistance films at the junction between the grid and the active material which reduces the charge-acceptance rate. Frequently, a battery with this type of construction can only be deeply cycled twenty or thirty times without damage, as opposed to over 200 times for a typical deep-cycle and up to 1800 cycles for a high-quality deep-cycle battery.

Carrying a starting or cranking battery on board a boat in most cases is not necessary, provided the system has ample capacity and is operated and charged properly. The actual number of amp-hours consumed during starting is small, so a dedicated engine-starting battery mostly goes along for a free ride, except for the cost in space, weight, and charging complexity. If you insist on a separate battery for starting only, then we recommend using a separate dedicated alternator and a separate battery switch.

## Capacity

The capacity of a battery is most influenced by the following factors: the rate of discharge, the practical limits of final voltage, the temperature of the battery, the amount of active material, the design and number of the plates, the volume and specific gravity of the electrolyte, and the age of the battery.

**DISCHARGE RATE.** The rate at which a battery is discharged dramatically affects the capacity. Deep-cycle battery capacities are typically given at the 20-hour rate. In other words, if a battery will give 5 amps for 20 hours, it has a 20-hour rating of 100 amp-hours. The 20-hour rate is useful because it tells you about how much power can be taken from a battery in a day. The following table illustrates the effect of higher discharge rates.

| Number of Hours for Discharge | Actual Capacity (Percent of Rating) |
|:---:|:---:|
| 20 | 100% |
| 10 | 89% |
| 5 | 78% |
| 3 | 66% |
| 1 | 45% |

**FINAL VOLTAGE.** The acceptable final battery voltage also figures in the battery capacity equation. If, for example, the equipment being operated stops working at 11.5 volts, that is the lowest limit to which the battery may be discharged, so a system with this criterion will have a smaller capacity. Some loads, like incandescent lighting for example, still operate at 10.5 volts. The engine starter may pull the battery all the way down to 9.5 volts and still have sufficient power for starting. The final voltage for tests of deep-cycle capacity is generally 10.5 volts.

**TEMPERATURE.** Temperature also affects the amp capacity of the battery. Batteries are comfortable at the same temperature humans are, 72 to 77 degrees Fahrenheit. At 120 degrees, the maximum temperature the battery should ever see, it will deliver up to 115 percent of its rating; however, its life will be shortened by perhaps 20 percent. At zero degree Fahrenheit, only 40 percent of the power is available, but it will have a very long life provided it does not freeze. These changes are due to the variation in the electrolyte's viscosity. When the temperature is higher, the electrolyte is able to diffuse easily; the opposite is true for low temperatures.

Temperature is important to monitor while charging. If the

batteries are warm to the touch, the internal temperature may be approaching the high limit of 120 degrees. Millions of batteries are killed due to excessive temperature from overcharging. Mercifully, this generally happens after the batteries have been "gassed" dry, so they were dead anyway. It pays to lay your hand on the batteries if they have been on a charger for some time. If they are warm and bubbling like a teakettle, you're killing them.

Temperature and specific gravity are related. The specific gravity of a battery indicates whether it is fully charged or not. When the battery is fully charged, there is more sulfuric acid in the water. Since the acid is denser than water, the specific gravity goes up to as high as 1.300 for battery electrolyte (the specific gravity of pure water is 1.000). If the specific gravity falls to around 1.100, the battery is fully discharged.

Some hydrometers used for measuring the battery electrolyte have a thermometer built in, and thus compensate for the temperature. If not, this rule can be used: a factor of .001 should be added to the reading for each 3 degrees above 77 F, or subtracted for every 3 degrees below 77 F.

**ACTIVE MATERIAL, PLATES, AND ELECTROLYTE.** The amount of active material, the design and number of plates, and the volume and specific gravity of the electrolyte affect the capacity of the battery also. There is not really much we can do about the first two, except choose our batteries carefully from a reputable manufacturer. The volume and specific gravity of the electrolyte we can vary, however.

If the specific gravity is increased, the capacity of the battery is increased. Like most benefits, this too carries a liability. This time it is increased corrosive attack on the plates that shortens life. This corrosive attack increases as the temperature rises. This is the reason that batteries used in the tropics usually have a lower specific gravity. The specific gravity of the electrolyte varies from 1.230 to 1.300, with the lower number common for deep-cycle batteries in tropical climates and the higher number typical in temperate climates for starting batteries. The most common electrolyte has a specific gravity of 1.265. If the electrolyte level is not maintained, not only is there the risk of damage to the battery, but there is also a loss of capacity because there is not enough electrolyte to sustain the chemical reaction. It is important to always make sure that the batteries are filled to the proper level, at least 1/4-inch above the plates.

**AGE.** The change in capacity of a battery as a function of age is very interesting. A new battery during its first cycle may not give its total capacity, but as it is cycled a few times, the capacity actually increases to its rating and perhaps 10 percent to 20 percent more. If the battery is of high quality, this increase will last for a long time and then begin a slow descent. Once the battery capacity reaches about 80 percent of its rating, the remaining capacity is lost much more quickly, and at this point the battery has lived its useful life.

An interesting point about the type of battery failures seen during the last ten years is that ten years ago, about 30 percent of failures were due to "mud" shedding off the plates and building up in the bottom of the battery and finally shorting out the cell. Today, only about 5 percent are due to mud build-up. New pastes contain various substances to increase their adhesive properties, and the grid design has advanced at the same time, helping to solve this problem. Improvements in the insulating barriers, called separators, between the positive and negative grids, have given more mechanical strength and electrical insulating value. Fiberglass and plastic technology have been instrumental in these advances.

Rather than age, the most common reason for battery failure today is poor charging techniques. Most batteries don't die— they are murdered. The second most common failure usually occurs at the connection of the most positive grid connection and the top of the grid. In other words, the battery is carrying most of its current in the top 20 percent of the grid because the battery charger is on all the time. To help this problem, engineers are now designing the plates with more lead in the upper part of the plate and less in the lower corners.

## Recovery and Mid-Capacity
Proper use of a storage battery not only affects its longevity but also the amount of power available. If the total kilowatt-hours

delivered by the battery throughout its life is plotted as a function of the percent of discharge, we find that it is at its maximum if the battery is discharged to the 50-percent point. This means that we get the most power for the least cost if the battery is discharged to the 50-percent point.

A battery is also able to deliver more power if it is used in an intermittent fashion. This is because a resting battery tends to recover. For example, if your car won't start and the battery is depleted to the point where it will not turn over the engine, give up for a while to let the battery recover and it will give you another chance. One of the reasons the battery has recovered is that the electrolyte has had time to diffuse, thus supplying fresh sulfuric acid to the plate surface. A battery will give 10 percent to 20 percent more power if it is used in an intermittent fashion. That is power you can use.

These two factors dictate a two-battery system. By using battery #1 today, and battery #2 tomorrow, we are able to take advantage of the resting recovery phenomenon and we are able to determine the 50-percent discharge point.

With a two-battery system and an accurate digital voltmeter, it is possible to determine the 50-percent discharge point simply and accurately. As previously noted, the at-rest, open-circuit voltage of a fully charged battery is about 12.6 volts. The at-rest, open-circuit voltage of a 50-percent discharged battery after 24 hours is about 12.2 volts. It is obvious that it requires a very accurate meter to measure this difference.

When the entire battery system is discharged to the 50-percent point, there is still ample cranking capacity to start all but the most difficult engines, again indicating that carrying a separate starting battery in most cases is not necessary.

**MID-CAPACITY PHILOSOPHY.** The mid-capacity usage philosophy requires that large capacity batteries be installed so that they are charged and discharged through the middle range of their capacity. There are several reasons for this, but one of the most important is that the charge-acceptance rate and the conversion efficiency is fairly high in the middle range of the capacity. To charge a battery to the 100-percent level requires a small charging current over a long period of time, and to deeply discharge any battery shortens its life. Operating in the battery's mid-capacity with periodic "conditioning" to bring the battery up to full charge ensures maximum power and life.

Let's take our example and see what the charge/discharge routine should be. Let's assume a 400 amp-hour system that is fully charged and has a daily load of 50 amps. After 4 days, the system will approach the 50-percent discharged point (4 days x 50 amp-hours = 200 amp-hours). If we assume an 80-percent efficiency during charging, then it will require 250 amps to fully recharge the battery.

The charge-acceptance rate for the first 150 to 200 amps will be fairly high. A 25-percent charge rate (100 amps) would be typical. As the battery voltage climbs toward the gassing point, the charge-acceptance rate drops, and it will require much longer at a lower current to put the remaining power back in the battery. Do we have to? We would like to avoid running the engine for a long time to put those last few amps back in. We can do that if the system is operating in its mid-capacity.

If the system is properly designed, the battery can be charged with a bulk current to about the 85-percent level quickly. This can be the regular charging routine. This means that the 400 amp-hour system is really a bit undersized, because we now have only 85 percent of our original capacity, or 340 amp-hours. So the 50-percent discharge point now only gives us 170 amp-hours of usable capacity.

What are we going to do? We have two choices: increase the capacity or decrease the load. If we wanted to maintain our 50 amp-hour load for 4 days and stay in the mid-capacity of the batteries, we would take the difference in capacity at 85 percent charged and 50 percent charged and set that equal to the amount of capacity that we wanted. In other words, 35 percent of the battery's capacity should be equal to the desired load (in our example, 200 amp-hours). This says we need a battery capacity of 571 amps to maintain this load and obey both the 50-percent discharge rule and the mid-capacity rule.

This would be an ideal design. We did not take into account the resting recovery phenomenon nor the benefits of auxiliary sources like solar panels. This is a power system that will carry the load with only two or three hours of engine running time every four days. To go on a little further with our example, suppose we had the required 571 amp-hour capacity to maintain our 200 amp-hour, 4-day load. Our normal charging procedure will be to charge quickly from the 50-percent to the 85-percent level. But can we always get back to the 85-percent level?

No. With each successive discharge, a bit more lead sulfate accumulates that cannot be removed during the normal bulk charging cycle. If this lead sulfate is allowed to accumulate, the structure becomes more and more rigid and well defined and much harder to remove by charging. That is the reason that periodic "conditioning" of the battery is absolutely essential for maximum capacity and long battery life.

Every thirty days, the batteries should be fully conditioned. This means that the batteries must be taken to their highest natural voltage with a small, controlled current.

Compromise is inescapable. The parameters we have given are based on engineering principles which are also based on compromises between theory and reality. Again, the question is what do you want to compromise? If you want the load, then you cannot compromise the resources required to meet that load.

## Charging

Field experience has proven that the typical battery charging system with constant voltage regulation set between 13.8 and 14.0 volts was woefully inadequate as a method of charging batteries, and nearly always results in reduced battery capacity and shortened battery life.

What is the solution? How can we charge batteries quickly, fully, and safely, and then maintain them in that condition without water consumption and deterioration? The points below summarize what research has revealed about how deep-cycle batteries should be charged in an ideal situation (see **Figure 3-3**).

**1.** Charging should begin when the battery reaches a 50-percent discharged state. This can be determined by checking the "at-rest voltage" (no load, no charge) after 24 hours. A 100-percent charge will have an at-rest voltage of about 12.6 to 12.7 volts. A 50-percent discharged battery will have an at-rest voltage of about 12.2 volts.

**Figure 3-3. Ideal Battery Charge/Discharge Curve**

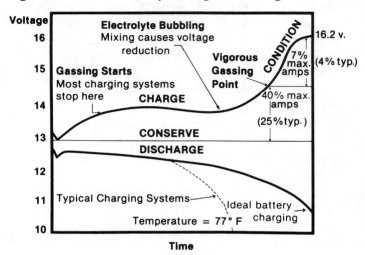

**2.** If the discharge state is unknown, begin charging with a current of up to 40 percent of the battery capacity (20-hour rate). If you know that the batteries are 50-percent discharged, then the charge rate should be about 25 percent of capacity.

**3.** When the batteries begin to vigorously gas, at about 14.4 to 14.6 volts, the current must be reduced. The battery is now about 75-percent to 85-percent charged.

**4.** To fully charge to the 85-percent level, reduce the current to 10 percent of the battery capacity and maintain it until the battery begins to gas.

**5.** To charge to the 100-percent level, reduce the current to 3 to 7 percent (4 percent is a good round number) of the battery capacity and maintain it until the voltage rises to its highest natural level with this conditioning current. This will be about 16.2 volts for a battery in good condition, and it will take three or four hours to reach it if the charging current is 4 percent of the real battery capacity.

The above parameters are for 12-volt batteries at 77 degrees F, with what would be considered a typical electrolyte.

## Buying and Installation Considerations

About the most seamanlike battery installation imaginable would consist of 6-volt deep-cycle batteries, with two batteries connected in series to make a 12-volt bank. There would be two banks, each able to deliver about 200 amps—over 400 amps available in a very compact space. Six-volt deep-cycle batteries are among the best batteries money can buy; very heavy construction is employed, and 6-volt batteries are not nearly as difficult to move around in the confines of a boat as the popular 8-D batteries are.

For the battery installation and distribution system from those batteries, we suggest these simple rules:

**1.** Install the batteries in an accessible location so that service is easy, and allow proper ventilation for cooling and gas venting (also leave some space *between* the batteries).

**2.** Hook only the main battery cables to the batteries and then run them to a battery switch located within six feet of the batteries. Install a distribution breaker in the feed for the distribution system as close as possible to the battery switch. All of the rest of the wiring should be supplied from the distribution system.

**3.** Secure the battery and their boxes so that even if the boat is turned upside down and shaken vigorously, the batteries will not move and acid will not spill.

Be sure to keep the tops of the batteries free of dirt, water, battery acid, and corrosion. Good maintenance, a thin coating of anti-corrosive spray, and catalytic battery caps can keep batteries clean and looking good for many years.

Catalytic caps are manufactured by Hydro-Cap Corporation. The hydrogen and oxygen gas given off by the battery is recombined catalytically in the cap to form water which then returns to the cell. Very little water is lost, and if the boat is turned over, the bilge will not be flooded with battery acid. Additional benefits are that there is no corrosive acid mist given off that causes the green stuff commonly found on battery terminals, and the explosive hydrogen/oxygen mix is greatly reduced. These caps can be made to fit nearly all batteries, but they require vertical space. If they can be installed, the problems they prevent are worth the expense.

The cables terminating on the battery should be bolted and have only one conductor per connection. All other positive connections should be made at the battery switch or in the distribution panel. The negative connections should be made on a negative bus. This type of installation makes terminal maintenance a snap.

Still worried about these batteries starting the engine? Will cranking current hurt deep-cycle batteries? No, it will not hurt the batteries, and the engine will start as if it were hooked up to a public utility. In a system like this, there are so many amps available that the batteries do not need a cranking rating; there is plenty of power.

Keep in mind when planning your battery installation that "paralleling" is not recommended. If you want more capacity, change to the two six-volt batteries in series system. Do not hang another battery on the system in parallel. It will work for a while, maybe two years, maybe three years. What happens, however, is a slow deterioration of the plates due to small circulating currents set up between the two batteries. Eventually a cell in one battery goes bad and it drags down the whole parallel bank. The charging system charges and charges, but the bad cell is robbing all the current, so the other cells do not get charged. The result? The good battery is destroyed as well.

This problem does not occur in a series system. Capacity can be matched to heavy demand by using 6-volt batteries in series that are as large as necessary. If you still need higher capacity, you'll have to step up to the world of large power systems and build it with individual two-volt cells.

Paralleling batteries has caused other problems. In at least one case that we know of, the side of one battery case was totally melted when one cell, in a system of five 8-Ds in parallel, shorted and the remaining cells supplied a huge amount of current to the shorted cell. It generated enough heat to destroy the battery case. The mess was horrible. The only good result of the experience was that the owner did not have to be convinced to abandon his parallel system.

## Other Battery Installation Considerations

The U.S. Coast Guard gives several guidelines for battery installation. They warn boatowners not to install electronic equipment or battery chargers above the batteries. The gases given off during charging consist mainly of hydrogen and oxygen. This is an explosive mixture and should not be introduced into an area where an electrical spark may cause an explosion.

In addition to the hydrogen and oxygen given off, the battery also releases small quantities of corrosive sulfide gases. These gases will destroy the sensitive electronic circuit boards in equipment installed over a battery.

The batteries should be located as high as practical in the boat, and as close to the engine starter as possible. Keeping batteries high and out of the bilge, insures they will be dry and ready on that horrible day when you are taking on water and have to call for help or depend on the bilge pump.

*   *   *

High-quality deep-cycle batteries are expensive. But when making battery choices, quality is what really counts. A good deep-cycle battery will not only last for years, if properly sized for your needs, it will also provide the performance to make your cruising safer and more enjoyable.

Your deep-cycle batteries deserve proper use, charging, and care. Long life and full capacity will be your reward. For further reading on the subject, we suggest *The Bullet-Proof Electrical System* by Rick Proctor, owner of Cruising Equipment Company, which specializes in the design of marine power systems ($4.95 from Cruising Equipment Co.; 6315 Seaview Avenue N.W.; Seattle, WA 98107).

# SELECTING A BATTERY CHARGER

We know how to charge batteries properly. But knowing how doesn't mean we can get it done—at least not easily.

The ideal battery charger would be multi-phased. Its first phase would be a charge mode during which it would drive a *constant current* into the batteries until they reach the vigorous gassing point, at about 14.4 to 14.6 volts. When this voltage is reached, the charger would go into a *constant voltage* mode, the second phase, maintaining the batteries at 13.0 to 13.2 volts.

About every thirty days, the charger would enter a phase to *condition* the batteries. In this phase, the charger would feed the batteries a constant current at about four percent of their capacity until battery voltage reached about 16.2 volts. This conditioning phase would ensure that the batteries could maintain full capacity and achieve a long battery life.

Currently there are no battery chargers on the marine market that allow the last phase of conditioning the batteries. Most of the battery chargers that are available choose to perform only one of the first two phases, providing either constant current or constant voltage and hence are compromises of the ideal.

Besides being characterized as constant-voltage or constant-current types, chargers are further classified by the method they use to rectify or convert the voltage from 120 volts AC to 12 volts DC, and by how they control or regulate the current and the phases of charging.

Let's first look at the different types.

## Minimal Chargers

The chargers of our nightmares are built to state-of-the-art, third-world specifications. They weigh about fifty pounds and have a knob that varies from one to ten. Ten, we assume, would cause a battery meltdown. They have voltmeters, ammeters, porcelain-insulated knife switches, and high-voltage, cone-shaped, insulated 12-volt output terminals. They look like something out of a Flash Gordon movie. What really terrifies us is that far too often, we find them lurking in engine rooms.

This nightmare battery charger is a simple, manually adjustable isolation step-down transformer, feeding a full-wave bridge rectifier, and then the battery. If the voltage and current are monitored almost constantly (in order to make appropriate adjustments) it will charge the battery without destroying it. That's the real challenge—not destroying the battery.

The third-world charger is a heavy duty version of the standard automotive battery charger. Nearly all inexpensive chargers are nothing more than a transformer to step the voltage down from 110 volts and a diode bridge to change it from alternating current to direct current.

Generally, even the cheapest of these have overcurrent protection such as an automatic reset circuit breaker. When the output current exceeds the rating of the breaker, it trips. Then a few seconds later, after it cools down, it automatically resets and the process is repeated. Hopefully, after a while, if the charger is not connected to too large a load, the battery will slowly charge up on the pulses it gets while the charger is on.

When the output current falls below the automatic breaker's rating, the charger stays on continuously. Gradually the battery becomes charged and the voltage increases to the limit set by the transformer ratio and the input voltage. If there is no load, the current drops and gradually becomes a trickle. The trickle continues while the battery voltage slowly rises perhaps as high as 15 volts and stays there until the battery dies.

If you must use a third-world charger, the best choice is to not leave the charger on all the time (the lesser of two evils). If the charger is *not* left on, sulfate is forming on the plate with self-discharge, but if the charger *is* left on, the battery will be destroyed from overcharging, excessive gassing, and loss of water. With this type of charger, maintaining the water level, particularly during a long charging period, is critical.

If the boat sits unused for long periods, the batteries must be charged at least once a month to make up for the 3-percent to 10-percent self-discharge of the battery. If the batteries are in daily service, they must be charged when the voltage drops to about 12.2 volts. You charge only for a few hours—all you have to do is replace what you have used.

As we know, batteries must be conditioned occasionally. Third-world chargers cannot perform this function, but if you leave the charger on for a longer period, say 24 hours, the battery voltage will increase to the highest output voltage of the charger. It may not be the required voltage to condition the batteries (16.0 to 16.2 volts) but it is the best you can do. Taking the batteries to the highest voltage of the charger insures that as much as possible of the available plate material is converted back into usable lead paste.

Third-world chargers were designed to charge a battery for engine starting, then be removed. Leaving them on continuously amounts to a death sentence for your batteries. But such premature battery death is preventable.

## Automatic Chargers

If you take all of the precautions for battery charging listed above, you will not only be a rare boatowner, you will also be the model for a reasonably good automatic battery charger.

The majority of automatic chargers on the market fall into two main categories: ferro-resonant or silicon-controlled rectifier (SCR) types. Ferro-resonant chargers (such as those made by Ratelco, Constavolt, Guest, Professional Mariner, and Newmar) use the design of the transformer, the configuration of its winding, and resonant capacitors to regulate the voltage and current delivered to the battery by controlling the magnetic field in the transformer. The important thing about these chargers is that the voltage is maintained at a constant level, typically around 13.8 volts. Some of these chargers have an additional circuit that turns the charger off at some level, say 14.0 volts, and back on at some differential voltage below that, generally about 1.1 to 1.5 volts below the turn-off or "drop-out" voltage. If this differential voltage is too small, the charger will cycle on and off too often, overcharging the battery and causing excessive gassing. If the differential is too large, the battery will never be fully charged.

The second main type is the SCR (silicon-controlled rectifier) charger. SCR chargers (made by Newmar, Dynamote, and a host of others) use a completely different electronic technique to accomplish battery charging. The battery terminal voltage is monitored and the SCRs (which are nothing more than diodes that can be turned on as needed) are turned on at a variable rate, shooting current into the battery. In this way, the battery is continuously pulsed with rectified DC power every time the SCR conducts. The SCR is fired or turned on by a regulator designed to maintain the battery at some average voltage. If the voltage falls, the SCRs are turned on more often. As the voltage rises, the rate is reduced. The fault with this type of charging is that there is no single voltage that is perfect for charging and maintaining batteries.

Comparing the advantages and disadvantages of these two major types of chargers gives no clear conclusion, as each has its virtues and vices. A ferro-resonant charger is generally larger and heavier than an SCR charger of the same rating. Ferro-resonant chargers make less electrical noise than the SCR type. Each time the SCRs fire, a "spike" is propagated through the power system. If radios are used while the AC system is on, there may be a hum or buzz interfering with the radio. This is one of the reasons the ferro-resonant charger is more popular than the SCR in the commercial marine market. When a commercial boat leaves port, an AC generator is started and kept running until she returns to port. The battery charger is left on continuously, and the full complement of DC equipment will be operating.

Since most pleasure boaters do not run their battery chargers while underway and using their radios, they seldom experience problems with the popular SCR chargers. The SCR charger is compact, easily controlled, and usually quite reliable, if components of sufficient rating are used.

The biggest problem with most SCR chargers is the design of the voltage regulator. Too bad for the batteries that the voltage of these chargers is a compromise voltage, just at the verge of gassing and well above what is an optimal "float" or "conserve" voltage. This combination results in a charger that takes a long time to charge the battery to the 13.8-volt level, and then shortens battery life by holding it at that level, on the verge of gassing.

## Choosing a Charger

During conversations with engineers who design battery chargers, we hear one refrain repeatedly—that the unique requirements of marine use make designing the best battery charger a difficult task. To appreciate the problem, consider the different jobs that the charger must accomplish.

Let's assume that we have a fully charged battery and use it to the 50-percent discharged level before we begin recharging. If we are using shore power to recharge, time may not be a consideration, but if we are using an auxiliary generator it well could be. If minimizing engine running time is the goal, then any charging rate lower than full output of the charger, or the full acceptance rate of the batteries, is not acceptable. All this implies a high-capacity, constant-current charger.

Sometimes, however, the boat and the batteries will sit unattended for months, during which the charger must not slaughter the batteries. These parameters require a precise constant-voltage float charge that can be set to match the battery manufacturer's specifications.

Finally, we need a charger which will *fully* charge the battery. When is a battery fully charged? The widely accepted procedure seems to be this: charge with a finish current rate as specified by the manufacturer until the voltage no longer rises and the specific gravity no longer increases. The finish rate is typically 3 percent to 7 percent of the battery capacity.

None of the chargers currently offered will do all these things. As you can see, without even considering such factors as age, temperature, moisture, vibration, and having different sizes or types of batteries on the same charger, the problem is much bigger than it first seems. So, choosing a charger boils down to which one will do the batteries the most good with the least harm. (Hopefully, the charger will also be reliable.)

We have made do with all of these chargers by employing tricks like installing time clocks to turn the charger on for one hour a day, or adding a voltage-sensing relay and turning the charger on and off as the battery cycles, or even turning the unit on and off manually.

A truly automatic battery charger would be one that can be left on continuously without excessive water consumption (less than a couple ounces per year per cell for a moderate battery system), one that will charge fast and will charge as fully as possible, and one that will do the least harm to the battery. Since there is no charger that performs totally in accordance with these requirements, the buyer has to decide which compromises will best suit his needs.

\* \* \*

In comparing chargers, it is important to note that the rated output of a charger is often misleading, since normally the voltage at which that output is supplied is so low as to be useless for most battery charging.

Many constant-voltage chargers will only supply their rated current well below 13.0 volts. Above that, the current quickly falls to practically nothing. Unless the battery is horribly discharged, very little battery charging occurs below 12.8 volts.

In contrast, a constant-current charger will still be delivering its rated output until the charging voltage limit is reached. Thus it will deliver much more energy in the same time. A 20-amp constant-current charger will often outperform a 40-amp constant-voltage unit.

## SHORE POWER SYSTEMS

The boating public has become accustomed to the conveniences of electrical appliances aboard their boats. However, there is often little thought given to the capacity of the boat's electrical system. The average boatowner simply plugs the appliance into a receptacle and expects it to work. Only when turning on an appliance causes the main AC breaker to trip, does he realize the electrical system is overloaded.

The following formulas have been developed by ABYC, (American Boat and Yacht Council, Inc.), as guidelines for determining the total AC power required on a given boat. Since a boat can be supplied by either a single or multiple shore power system, the load calculations in **Figure 3-4** allow for "Leg A" and "Leg B" in order that the electrical power may be split between two separate systems when the load exceeds the amperage capacity of the single system. On a 50-ampere, 125/250-volt system, the load can be more evenly split between the two ungrounded conductors, each carrying 125 volts.

With the increased popularity of air conditioning aboard

# Figure 3-4: ABYC Electrical Load Calculation Formulas

**A.** Lighting Fixtures and Receptacles. Length times width of living space, times 3 watts per square foot, (exclude spaces exclusively for machinery or for open deck space).
Formula: Length x width x 3 = _____ lighting watts.

**B.** Small Appliances (Galley and Dinette Areas). Number of circuits times 1,500 watts for each 20 ampere appliance receptacle circuit.
Formula: Number of circuits x 1,500 = _____ small appliance watts.

**C.** Total
Formula: Lighting watts + small appliance watts = _____ total watts.

**D.** Load Factor
Formula: First 3,000 watts at 100% = _____
Remaining total watts x 35% = _____
Total watts divided by system voltage = _____ amperes.

**E.** Lighting and small appliance current (amperes) for each leg as calculated in "D" above:

|  | Leg A | Leg B |
|---|---|---|
|  | _____ | _____ |

**F.** Add nameplate amperes for motor and heater loads:

|  | Leg A | Leg B |
|---|---|---|
| Exhaust and supply fans | _____ | _____ |
| Air conditioners* ** | _____ | _____ |
| Electric, gas or oil heaters* (25% of largest motor in above items) | _____ | _____ |
| Sub-Total | _____ | _____ |

*Omit smaller of these two, except include any motor common to both functions.
**If system consists of 3 or more independent units, adjust the total by multiplying by 75% diversity factor.

**G.** Add nameplate amperes at indicated use factor percentage for:

|  | Leg A | Leg B |
|---|---|---|
| Disposal (10%) | _____ | _____ |
| Water Heater (100%) | _____ | _____ |
| Wall-mounted Ovens (75%) | _____ | _____ |
| Cooking units (75%) | _____ | _____ |
| Refrigerator (100%) | _____ | _____ |
| Freezer (100%) | _____ | _____ |

Ice Maker (50%)          _____    _____
Dishwasher (25%)          _____    _____
Washing Machine (25%)     _____    _____
Dryer (25%)               _____    _____
Trash Compactor (10%)     _____    _____
Air Compressor (10%)      _____    _____
Battery Chargers (100%)   _____    _____
(Other) _____          _____    _____

_____                  _____    _____
            Sub-Total      _____    _____
**Adjusted Sub-Total       _____    _____

**If four or more appliance are installed, adjust the total by multiplying by 75% diversity factor.

**H.** Add amperes for free standing range as distinguished from separate oven and cooking units as provided for in above list. Determine this from the following table. Divide watts by 125 volts or 250 volts, depending on which unit is installed.

| RANGE | |
| --- | --- |
| NAMEPLATE WATTS | USE (WATTS) |
| 10,000 or less | 80% or rating |
| 10,001 - 12,500 | 8,000 |
| 12,501 - 13,500 | 8,400 |
| 13,501 - 14,500 | 8,800 |
| 14,501 - 15,500 | 9,200 |

                          Leg A      Leg B

_____  Sub-Total           _____

**I.** Add previously determined values:

Lighting and
Small Applicances (**E.**)   _____    _____
Motors (**F.**)              _____    _____
Fixed Appliances (**G.**)    _____    _____
Free Standing Range (**H.**) _____    _____

        **TOTAL**            _____    _____

NOTE: If the total for legs A and B are unequal, use the larger value to determine the power required.

boats, many boatbuilders have elected to provide a separate shore power system (or branch circuit) for the air conditioning. In small boats, a single 30-amp system is adequate for lighting and small appliances, but insufficient to carry the load of an air conditioning unit. By splitting the system into two legs with one shore power cord supplying power to the air conditioning equipment, and the other providing service to the boat's other AC equipment, each system gives the boat uninterrupted AC electrical service.

After performing the load calculations in Figure 3-4, you may realize that it will be necessary to either split the system and balance the load, or to add an additional AC system to handle the air conditioning.

## 110-VOLT ELECTRICAL SYSTEM INSTALLATION

The source of power for your boat's alternating current (AC) electrical system can be either a shoreside connection or an on-board AC electrical generator. This system provides electricity for appliances and fixed AC electrical equipment aboard the boat. While the principles of electric theory are the same whether on shore or afloat, the conductors and the methods of conductor installation differ considerably from those used shoreside.

Because of color-coding and polarity requirements, working with your boat's AC electrical system is really not complicated. A grounding conductor, or ground wire, in an AC system is always green. The neutral wire or grounded conductor is white. The ungrounded conductor, or "hot" wire, is identified by any color other than green or white and is usually black or red.

ABYC standards require that marine AC electrical systems be "polarized." A polarized system is one in which the hot and neutral wires are connected in the same relation to all terminals on all devices in the circuit.

For example, receptacles are connected so that the neutral wire attaches to the terminal identified by the letter "S", normally a silver color. The hot wire should be attached to the brass or copper terminal. The grounding wire, green, is to be attached to the ground terminal on the receptacle. This procedure insures that the proper polarity is maintained and that the electricity will "flow" safely, without restriction, through each circuit. Terminal screws are color coded for easy identification.

In all marine electrical applications, keeping the components dry and free from the accumulation of moisture is of prime importance. Junction boxes, receptacles, panelboards and other enclosures in which electrical connections are made should be weatherproof or installed in a protected location. All current-carrying conductors should be routed as far away as practical from areas where water may accumulate.

The black, white and green ground conductor in each cable or cord used in marine applications must each be of *stranded* wire. Household conductors, on the other hand, have a single, solid-core wire. The number of strands required in each conductor in marine applications is directly related to the conductor's diameter and the degree to which the wire will be subjected to flexing through movement or vibration. The conductor's proper size and diameter is also determined by the demand or amount of current the conductor must carry.

Good household wiring often travels through the house in metallic tubing called conduit. The conduit supports and protects the wires within the walls and ceiling of your home. But on your boat, conductors are supported throughout their length by a self-draining loom or are secured every 18 inches by straps or clamps. In areas other than the machinery compartments of your boat, nonmetallic straps or clamps are ideal for holding conductors firmly in place. Metal clamps lined with an insulating material to minimize damage from chafing are used in engine rooms and machinery areas.

Another major difference between household wiring and the AC electrical wiring aboard your boat occurs when two conductors or wires are joined together, or a conductor is connected to a terminal on an appliance, receptacle or circuit breaker. A common practice in household wiring is to splice wire to wire by means of electrical tape or wire nuts. Wire nuts or twist-on connectors have no place aboard a boat.

Joining conductor to conductor in marine applications is best accomplished through the use of insulated, solderless crimp-on

## Figure 3-5. Tools and Supplies for Electrical Wiring

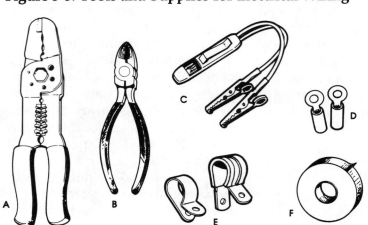

Illustrated here are some of the basic tools and supplies that make wiring aboard a boat an easy task. In addition to the items shown, you may have occasion to use an electric drill and a saber saw, particularly if you are adding another shore power circuit or a new receptacle.

**A. Multipurpose Tool.** This tool allows the insulation to be easily stripped from wires without damaging the wire conductors. The same tool is used to cut wire and to crimp the insulated, solderless connectors on the wire. For optimum connections, the crimping tool should be compatible with the insulated connector (tool and connector from the same manufacturer).

**B. Wire Cutters.** This form of pliers is strictly used for cutting wire conductors. Their shape and design makes them ideal for performing clean, even cuts of multi-stranded marine wire.

**C. Tester.** To check that all current is off before you begin to work on AC electrical items, be sure you have a voltage tester.

**D. Crimp-on Connectors.** Available in a variety of wire and stud sizes, these connectors crimp on to multi-stranded wire and fasten securely to the terminal screws of receptacles and breakers.

**E. Cable Clamps and Support Clips.** Available in nylon or metal with rubber insulation, cable clamps are used to support wiring (wiring should be supported every 18 inches to prevent unnecessary flexing).

**F. Electrical Tape.** It is a good practice to apply electrical tape around the wire and the insulation of the crimp-on connector to prevent moisture from entering the connection. Electrical "tracer" tape comes in a variety of colors and is an effective means of identifying various circuits during installation.

connectors. The crimp-on connection may be covered with electrical tape but under no circumstances should electrical tape be used to join two conductors together. Besides assuring continuity of current, crimp-on connectors prevent the conductors from being pulled apart when flexed.

Working with a boat's electrical system is something many boatowners refuse to do because they consider it mysterious. More than any other system on your boat, the AC electrical system is standardized. By having the proper tools (see **Figure 3-5**), following the safety tips outlined earlier and using marine electrical equipment, installing your own shore power system is relatively simple.

# 4

# The Steering System

## A TILLER OR A WHEEL?

A properly designed and installed wheel steering system should make a boat steer easier than with a tiller; the larger the boat the greater the improvement. To the ease of wheel steering, add the subtle but substantial satisfaction of standing tall at the helm, and it becomes clear why this type of steering has become the preference in sailboats down to about 30 feet and even smaller. As the racing sailor knows, a wheel is not as sensitive or responsive as a tiller, but at the same time, big boats and cruising boats do not want or need the ultimate sensitivity. What is desirable in a racing boat can be a source of effort on a cruising boat.

Then there are some often overlooked benefits from wheel steering. A wheel lets a boat be steered like the familiar automobile or bicycle: turn the way you want to go, not the opposite as with a tiller. A novice behind a wheel does not have to unlearn anything; at a tiller there is much to relearn. A 15,000-pound boat with a wheel can be steered by a child, but the same boat with a tiller will steer the child.

Some sailors argue that the pedestal and wheel obstruct the cockpit. They do (for that matter, the mast obstructs the deck); so does a tiller, however, especially when it needs to be swung in an arc. The point is, which is more important to the basic function of a boat, the convenience of an unobstructed cockpit or the necessity of an efficient way to steer her?

There is rarely justification for the typical wheel steering system in sailboats under about 27 feet or so. The cost is high relative to the benefits. Similarly, even larger, lightweight high-performance boats are likely to be better off with a tiller. The purists may scoff at the alternatives to a tiller, but chances are they are either hotshot racing types or they have docile, balanced boats that do not try to dislocate the shoulder on a broad reach in a breeze.

If you are considering buying a boat with wheel steering or retrofitting an existing boat, there are two primary factors to keep in mind: location and accessibility. The location of the wheel and the pedestal is one of the most common flaws in cockpit and deck layout. The steering station on smaller boats and cruising boats should let the helmsman reach the genoa sheet winches and the mainsheet. It is common to put the helmsman as far aft as possible on a racing boat. With the size of a racing crew, the helmsman needs to be out of the way, have the action in front of him, and be able to maintain his concentration. On a cruising boat, however, few helmsmen devote all of their attention to steering. The cruising sailor often sails alone or shorthanded, and most enjoy being amid the crew and able to stay in touch with what is going on belowdecks. That, in our opinion, means a wheel mounted well forward in the cockpit.

Finally, the accessibility of the components under the cockpit sole is just as important as the location of the components above. As boat buyers and owners, we demand that the engine be accessible, but we probably have not been as adamant as we should be about the accessibility of the components of wheel steering systems. These components need to be reachable for regular inspection, lubrication, adjustment of tension, and ultimately to permit repairs.

## Additional Considerations

While the advantages of pedestal steering are well known, the disadvantages of locating the compass atop the pedestal are not commonly understood and rarely acknowledged. Perhaps the greatest disadvantage is that the helmsman must completely remove his gaze from ahead to look downward at a considerable angle, as much as 60 degrees below horizontal. It may be good neck exercise, but it can be very inconvenient at times.

If there was a way to mount the compass higher, just below eye level, without jeopardizing its safety, the location would be nearly ideal. Furthermore, there is less magnification of the card from viewing it as a standing helmsman does, than if his line of sight passed through nearly a full diameter of the sphere, as from a sitting position. Looking down into the compass requires a bent-over forward lubberline and the attendant nuisance of some parallax error from standing vertical as the boat heels.

Pedestals can amplify the effects of engine vibration, the shuddering of the hull in a steep sea, the flexing of the sole from the crew moving about the cockpit, and the shock caused when the pedestal itself is used as a brace in rough going. The result can be damage to the pivot or jewel inside the compass, damage which may not be detected soon enough.

Finally, there is a strong trend toward putting arrays of instruments in pods near the compass. Instruments with meter movements, as in an analog display of boat speed or wind speed, have magnets inside, and these instruments are frequently positioned within 12 inches of the compass. The resulting deviation is correctable, but it is not possible to compensate for the varying amperage they handle.

In short, if you will be commissioning a new boat, you should consider the advantages of wheel steering. You should also, however, consider the alternatives to the pedestal for the location of the steering compass (for a more thorough examination of pedestal compasses, see Volume I, *Outfitting*, pages 119-122).

# TILLER-MOUNTED AUTOPILOTS

Autopilots are near the top of every sailor's wish list because they can make passagemaking so much less tedious. It's not much fun to be stuck at the tiller with your eyes glued to the compass when sailing in limited visibility or when motoring over long distances.

While the advantages of an autopilot are marked, not all autopilots are created equal. Furthermore, there are some things that no autopilot can do. For example, an autopilot can't see obstructions or other boats; they're not for daysailing in crowded areas or restricted waters. Autopilots perform best while reaching; they don't sail upwind with the skill of an experienced helmsman. Downwind, they are even worse; they can't see or respond to breaking waves or unusual wave patterns. The stronger the breeze, the poorer an autopilot performs.

## Features

The earliest marine autopilots were introduced in the 1930s. They operated on the principle of "hunting," where the pilot would continually steer the boat back and forth, hunting for the desired heading. This caused a zig-zag course, and required that the pilot be in continual motion, which made for more power consumption and wear and tear on the entire steering system.

**DEADBAND.** In the 1940s, the problem of hunting was solved by the introduction of a deadband into autopilot design. The deadband extends to either side of the pilot's assigned course. Within this deadband, the helm is inactive; the pilot only kicks in when the boat gets far enough off course to exceed the limits of the deadband.

On most modern autopilots, the deadband can be adjusted to allow for the natural yawing of the boat's course. This is often called a "seastate" control. Some pilots have infinite adjustment, others have a few prescribed settings. Some have wider deadband than others. For example the Plastimo AT50 can only be set with a deadband of either 6 degrees or 14 degrees; the Tillerpilot 1600 can be set through a range of 4 to 35 degrees.

**PROPORTIONAL CORRECTION/PROPORTIONAL RATE.** Most modern autopilots also utilize proportional correction. The pilot arm moves in proportion to the number of degrees off course. The farther off course, the farther the arm moves. It doesn't move faster, however. That's an additional feature called proportional rate, and only found on the more expensive autopilots for wheel steering. On some pilots, like the Autohelm 2000, the amount of proportional correction is adjustable.

**TRIM CONTROL.** The better autopilots offer trim control. When a change in wind velocity changes the trim of the boat, the helm may need to be set further off centerline to keep the boat on course. All pilots will apply some correction when the boat goes off course, but that correction may not be sufficient to return to the original course. A pilot with trim control senses that the proportional correction hasn't done the job, and adds more correction until the boat returns to course.

**OTHER FEATURES.** Trim control won't detect deviations off course caused by current or leeway. For that you need a Loran interface. Some pilots can also be directed by a windvane sensor, which steers a boat to a designated apparent-wind angle instead of to a compass course. According to the many owners of autopilots with this option, steering usually is not as satisfactory with the vane as when directed by compass.

Some tiller-mounted autopilots also have an off-course alarm, which beeps when the boat fails to return to within 15 degrees of course. Remote control is another common option, allowing you to steer the boat from the protection of the companionway dodger in inclement weather.

## Mechanics

All tiller-mounted autopilots are driven by a mechanical screw, which pushes or pulls an arm attached to the tiller. The differences between the various makes of tiller pilot are a function of how well, or how poorly, information is transmitted to the mechanical arm, and how well it responds to guide the boat.

**SPEED.** The amount and speed of the reaction varies. Some mechanical arms are more powerful or faster than others. For example, the arm on some autopilots moves at a rate of more than three centimeters per second, while others crawl along at less than one centimeter per second.

**WATERPROOFING.** Because the arm must move in and out of a casing, tiller-mounted autopilots are almost impossible to make waterproof. There are various ways that manufacturers attempt to seal the units. Some use O-rings and grease; others use formed gaskets to give a larger bearing surface for a better seal. The most expensive solution, and probably the most waterproof, is the use of a bellows for the entire length of the pilot arm. The bellows, however, can eventually collect water, and there is always possibility of a puncture.

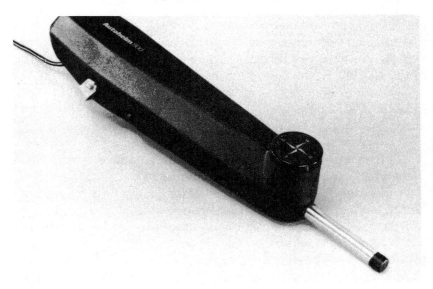

*The Autohelm 800 is typical of tiller mounted autopilots.*

The more controls an autopilot has, the greater the chance of water getting into the unit. Some autopilots have most of their controls operated by a membrane keypad, which does not violate the watertight integrity of the case. Despite their reputation for quitting when soaked, in a recent *Practical Sailor* reader survey, tiller-pilot owners indicate that about 95 percent of the time, the newer autopilots still run after being doused.

**COMPASS**. Although it's hidden inside the autopilot casing, nearly all pilots use a simple magnetic compass—a magnetic card in a bowl of liquid. The only difference between it and your ship's compass is that its card is marked with a code read by photo cell. The more reliable ones are lit by a light-emitting diode rather than a bulb. The disadvantage of these magnetic compasses is their small size and their susceptibility to deviation from metal objects and other compasses aboard your boat.

A better system, at least theoretically, is to use a fluxgate compass. This type of compass is the thing of the future. Instead of a floating magnetic card, a fluxgate compass senses the relative position of the earth's magnetic field with a stationary electromagnetic device. It has no moving parts, and has the potential for greater accuracy and speed with less power consumption. The use of fluxgate compasses is the big selling point of some of the newer autopilot models.

**FEEDBACK.** There are several different ways in which an autopilot can process the information it gets from its compass. The simplest to design is a system of mechanical feedback. Autopilots with this type of feedback are recognized by compass dials which rotate as the pilot arm moves.

Mechanical feedback requires a lot of moving parts and, hence, has a greater potential for breakdowns. For example, the Tillermaster operates and is calibrated with a series of pulleys and strings. It should be noted, however, that the potential for problems doesn't mean that problems will arise. The aforementioned reader survey showed the Tillermaster to be one of the more reliable autopilots.

The second type of feedback is analog. Through the use of circuitry, it eliminates many of the moving parts. It does not operate on strings or springs, so it should, in theory, be more durable. Once designed, it should also cost less to produce. Analog feedback allows for the addition of more features. The Plastimo and Tillerpilot are examples of this type of autopilot.

Digital feedback through the use of microprocessor technology is the latest craze in electronic engineering, and autopilot design is no exception. Digital feedback uses the same number of moving parts as analog feedback, and has far more complicated electronics, yet it offers the possibility of better accuracy.

**POWER.** The modern autopilot is energy-efficient. It's rare that one would require the installation of another battery. Still, they are not as energy-efficient as some manufacturers would have you believe. Be skeptical of the power consumption specifications provided by the manufacturer. For example, the manufacturer of one tiller-mounted autopilot claims an average power consumption of only 0.4 amps for its new model. At that rate, the pilot would be able to run for almost 100 hours off a typical ship's battery. Yet in our laboratory tests, we found that it consumed 0.43 amps when simply turned on, not moving. The consumption jumped to 0.85 amps when moving with no load, and to 1.2 amps when working against a 15-pound load.

As evidenced by this example, power consumption jumps dramatically with increased load. It follows that a more powerful autopilot will be more efficient under load. The speed and accuracy of an autopilot also play a role in its energy-efficiency. A "smarter" pilot will have to work less.

**INSTALLATION.** Installing a tiller-mounted autopilot is far simpler than installing an autopilot for wheel steering. Our survey indicated that tiller pilot installation is a two- to three-hour job for most boatowners; the installation of an autopilot for wheel steering, especially systems mounted belowdecks, is usually a job for a professional.

Nearly all tiller-mounted autopilots require mounting on the starboard side of the cockpit. The pilot casing pivots on a socket which is mounted on the coaming or cockpit seat; the pilot arm sits on a pin set into the tiller. Twelve-volt DC power must also be run to the autopilot's receptacle in the cockpit.

The autopilot must be mounted a specific distance off the boat's centerline, and a specific distance forward from the rudder post (or the pintles, in the case of an outboard rudder). It is a rare boat where you can line both mounting points in a horizontal plane. Most often, a bracket must be fitted on the tiller to accommodate the pilot's mounting requirements. Don't try to install your new autopilot two hours before you are scheduled to leave on a long cruise. You may find that you have to order a tiller bracket, extension for the pilot arm, or a pedestal or cantilever bracket for the pilot case to make it fit correctly.

As a final note of caution, autopilot operation is affected by VHF interference. Don't transmit from a powerful handheld VHF held within six feet of an operating autopilot.

# AUTOPILOTS FOR WHEEL STEERING

There are many things to consider when buying an autopilot for wheel steering, but the one to consider most cautiously is manufacturer hype. As with any type of sophisticated electronics, it's easy to be led astray by technical jargon and the boasts of the manufacturer. To fathom some autopilot brochures takes a degree in electrical engineering. One brochure, for example, says: "...systems employ solid state pulse width modulated amplifier stages to drive electro mechanical or electro hydraulic power units for precise and efficient positioning of the steering gear." What they mean is they use an amplifier that makes itself efficient by only pushing as hard as it has to. The same manufacturer boasts that theirs is the only autopilot with proportional rate. Not true; all the expensive pilots are proportional rate.

Another manufacturer tries to woo its customers by touting their compass as a "magnetometer," which they claim is superior to a fluxgate compass because it's not affected by changes in temperature. They say that some fluxgates vary up to 10 degrees with a temperature change of 10 degrees C. More baloney. A magnetometer *is* a fluxgate by definition. We've never heard of such wild variations with any fluxgate/magnetometer. To top that, the same manufacturer says its compass can "handle up to 1,000 degrees of change per second." Assuming that was true, what relevance would it possibly have for a sailboat?

Autopilot manufacturers often claim astoundingly low power consumption specifications; and some manufacturers seem to be more confused than their customers. One manufacturer was under the impression that there are 100 milliamps in an amp (there are 1000); so their power consumption specifications were off by a factor of ten. Another's specifications changed every time we talked to them.

Fortunately, it is possible to make some sense out of all the hoopla. Here are some of the pertinent points to consider.

### Above or Belowdecks?

Wheel-mounted autopilots can be divided into two categories: those mounted belowdecks and those mounted in the cockpit. If you want to go cheap, go for the above-deck variety. You'll save a lot money—perhaps thousands of dollars—but you'll pay a price in other ways.

First, you won't get comparable performance. Even the best performing above-deck, or "cockpit" autopilot, won't steer as well as the worst of the belowdecks pilots, according to a *Practical Sailor* reader survey.

Cockpit-mounted autopilots don't offer the same flexibility, either. They attach directly to a hub fitted to the steering wheel. To alter their speed to fit your boat's steering characteristics, you need to change the size of the hub. At the time of this writing, only the CPT pilot offers different size hubs. The gearing of a belowdecks pilot is flexible; you usually have several different drive systems to choose from, and a number of linkages from the drive system to the rudder post.

It's rare to find an autopilot that is truly waterproof. This makes most cockpit-mounted autopilots of limited use for bluewater cruising. Belowdecks autopilots, on the other hand, are protected from the elements. The only component that needs to be waterproof is the cockpit control station.

Some people consider autopilots a hazard to safety. It goes without saying that an autopilot is intended for uncrowded, open-water sailing; anyone who uses it otherwise is asking for trouble. If you have to grab the wheel in an emergency you don't want to fight with the pilot for control of the boat. With a cockpit-mounted autopilot you might win the battle, but many of the belowdecks units are stronger than you are. You have to disengage the pilot clutch first, which is no problem as long as you have a few extra seconds to spare.

In one way, a belowdecks autopilot can actually add safety. To do so, it has to bypass the existing steering cables and linkage, and attach directly to the rudder post. Then if the primary steering fails you have an independent backup. This can be a lifesaver should a steering cable break or jump a quadrant, for example. Edson, the premier manufacturer of steering systems, says they would not recommend the installation of an autopilot any other way.

You also get more convenience with a belowdecks autopilot; that is, after you go through the considerable grief of installation. A cockpit pilot has the drive and accompanying belts in the cockpit and underfoot. One *Practical Sailor* reader complained that his cat got its tail caught in the belt. The autopilot must be disassembled when not in use lest it be stolen. While this chore is admittedly simple with most units, you're still stuck with an unsightly hub permanently mounted on the steering wheel.

## Features

Cockpit-mounted autopilots for wheel steering share many of the same features as the tiller-mounted autopilots. They move at a constant speed, the amount of movement in proportion to the number of degrees off course (proportional correction). To keep the pilot from consuming too much power, a deadband is used. It extends either side of the pilot's assigned course. Within the deadband, the pilot is inactive. The deadband is either manually or automatically adjusted to allow for a normal amount of yaw. Feedback to control these features can either be mechanical, analog, or digital. Mechanical feedback may be tried and true, but it's also outdated and cumbersome. Digital is the wave of the future; its sophisticated electronics offers the promise of better accuracy and more features than analog circuitry.

Belowdecks autopilots are completely different from the cockpit-mounted variety, however. With few exceptions, manufacturers have discarded the deadband/proportional correction system of operation. Instead, they use the more advanced proportional rate system, with either digital or analog feedback.

Proportional rate means that an autopilot has variable speed. The variation in speed is proportional to how far and how fast the boat is being pushed off course. If the autopilot is just a few degrees off, the correction is slow and minimal. For this reason, a deadband isn't needed; nevertheless, many autopilots still have a "filter" to allow the boat some amount of natural yawing without pilot correction. Manufacturers claim that power consumption is less with proportional rate, because the system never lets the boat get far enough off course to need a forceful correction of the helm.

Trim control is common on all modern autopilots, whether they be above or belowdecks. When a change in wind velocity alters the trim of the boat, trim control adjusts the position of the helm to compensate. This helps the autopilot handle weather helm; without it the boat can round up in a gust of wind.

Most pilots can also be fitted with a remote control, attached via wire to the main control station. This is often called a "dodging" device, and aptly so, as its real value is to allow you to steer or dodge other boats from the protection of the companionway dodger. Just as commonplace is the ability to be controlled by windvane or Loran interface. A windvane is supposed to steer the boat by apparent-wind angle; which should be valuable when sailing upwind in a shifty breeze. Unfortunately, our survey showed that piloting by vane was rarely superior to piloting by compass, no matter what the type of autopilot.

As for Loran interfacing, manufacturers claim that it is much improved in recent years. That's because of the standardization of interfaces, and Loran features like waypointing, cross-track error, and speed and heading outputs which have become commonplace. Supposedly gone are the days when a Loran-directed autopilot would weave back and forth across a course like a drunk driver. According to manufacturers, it's important to have a standard "0180 data interface" on both the Loran receiver and the pilot. It is also important for the Loran to have the above mentioned features, in order to give the autopilot intelligent information.

## Installation

Installing a cockpit-mounted autopilot is a breeze compared to a belowdecks autopilot. A boatowner should be able to install a Tillermaster or First Mate cockpit pilot in two hours; after all, they're only modified tiller pilots.

A belt-driven system like the Autohelm 3000, CPT or Navico 4000, should take closer to four hours to install. Their drive units mount on a bracket that is screwed or clamped to either the pedestal or the cockpit seat. A hub is attached with U-bolts to the steering wheel. It's crucial to get the hub centered on the steering wheel, or the belt will have uneven tension. Too little or uneven tension can cause it to slip.

Installing an autopilot belowdecks is best left to the professional, but get an estimate on the job before you have him start. Otherwise, you may be in for quite a shock when the bill arrives. Professionally done, the job for a 35-foot boat is likely to cost from a minimum of several hundred dollars to a few thousand dollars, depending on how difficult the job is. Remember, this doesn't include the price of the pilot itself. And don't think it will be any cheaper for a smaller boat. It's likely to cost more, as the cramped confines of a small boat are more difficult to work in.

Boatbuilders can make it a lot easier on those who install

pilots by doing three things during construction. First, they can leave enough space around the rudder post so that the autopilot can be installed without having to have customized fittings fabricated at the yard or ordered from the steering system manufacturer. Second, they could mold a shelf into the hull adjacent to the post on which to mount the pilot drive.

Finally, they could lengthen the keyway, or "notch," which is machined into the rudder post for the primary steering system. An extra long keyway makes it easy to attach the autopilot linkage to the rudder post. If there isn't enough keyway for solid mounting, the rudder must be dropped and the keyway remachined, a significant added expense. To save money, set screws can be used in lieu of a keyway to attach the fittings to the rudder post, but they don't give as secure a fastening.

## Linear Versus Rotary Drive

Except for the rare sailboat with hydraulic steering, the choice for an autopilot drive is either linear or rotary. Linear drive utilizes a ram which is pushed or pulled by a screw, similar in concept to that of a tiller pilot. Rotary drive utilizes a chain or belt to turn the rudder. Both cockpit and belowdecks pilots are available in both versions.

A cockpit-mounted autopilot with linear drive is essentially a jury-rigged tiller pilot. The ram attaches directly to the steering wheel, but it can only turn the wheel through half of a revolution. The slow speed and limited turning range of these pilots put them at a marked disadvantage to rotary cockpit pilots.

In a belowdecks autopilot, rotary drive is commonly linked to the existing steering gear. However, the chain can be rigged directly to the rudder post. On some units, the chain can be eliminated by linking the drive to the rudder with a rack and pinion system.

Both linear and rotary drive autopilots have their advantages. Rotary drive is less expensive, but it's usually more difficult to install. This means that the initial savings are often wiped out by the installation costs. Whether rotary drive is cost-effective will depend on the design of your particular boat.

Some linear drives add considerable "drag" to the feel of the helm when steering by hand rather than by autopilot. That's because most linear drives are permanently attached to the rudder. Even when the pilot is turned off, the linear ram still has to move in and out as you turn the wheel. At least one unit solves this problem through the use of a mechanical clutch which disconnects the drive from the rudder when not in use, leaving the helm to turn without restriction.

## Compasses

At some risk of oversimplifying, autopilot compasses can be divided into two types, mechanical and electronic. Realize that within both types there is a wide range in quality; therefore it is impossible to state that one type is always superior.

A mechanical compass uses a compass card floating in liquid. In an autopilot, that card is usually read with an optical device. As is the case with many of the tiller-mounted autopilots, this "tried and true" type of compass is used in several of the cockpit-mounted models. In belowdecks autopilots, only a few manufacturers are still hanging on to this older technology. An electronic compass is commonly called a fluxgate or magnetometer, a stationary electromagnetic device that senses position relative to the earth's magnetic field.

In between the mechanical and the electronic compass is the Hall-effect compass. A Hall-effect device senses the presence or absence of a magnet. A compass with these devices still uses a rotating card. The greater the number of Hall-effect devices, the greater the potential accuracy.

Whether a compass is electronic or mechanical, it's still affected by a boat's motion. To minimize the effect of motion it has to be gimballed and mounted as low and as close to amidships as possible. Here, the belowdecks pilots have a big advantage, as they all have compasses separate from the control unit. This allows them to be mounted in the cabin for better stability. Theoretically, an electronic compass is less affected by motion than a mechanical one.

It's difficult to state that one autopilot's compass is better than another. Certainly the fluxgate has the potential to be better, but there are so many variations on the design of a compass that definitive comparison is nearly impossible. Before making a selection, talk to the owners of boats similar to yours. Seek out the advice of a reliable installer, not just an electronics salesman or manufacturer's representative. A good installation can maximize the performance of any wheel pilot; a poor installation can ruin the performance of even the best.

# 5

# Commissioning
# the New Engine

One has to assume that the boatowner who has installed his own engine will have (or will have acquired) sufficient mechanical expertise to follow a logical checkout and servicing procedure. On the other hand, the owner who has purchased a new boat or has had a new engine installed by a boatyard or engine dealer, can only assume that all the technical procedures have been performed by the installer before the installation was turned over to him. We'll concentrate, therefore, on the procedures and checks that the less-than-mechanically-sophisticated boatowner can use to ensure a satisfactory and long-lived association with his new power plant.

## INBOARD ENGINES

Up to a point, the new-engine commissioning procedure is the same for all inboards, both gas and diesel.

### Shaft Alignment
Proper engine and shaft alignment is a relatively simple matter, but one that many boatowners find intimidating. As a result, owners often complain of the effects of excessive engine vibration, but avoid checking the most common cause due to the erroneous belief that it is a complicated job.

Improper engine alignment works both ways from the shaft coupling. It can produce excessive vibration and wear, on the engine, its mounts, and its bearings. In the other direction, it can result in the rapid wear of the shaft and its bearings, and place excessive strains on the strut and even the hull itself. At worst, this can result in the shaft being thrown from the boat, or in the strut being torn from the hull, either of which creates a large opening in the hull, sinking the boat. At the very least, an improperly aligned shaft will shorten engine life, cut engine efficiency and RPM, and cause unnecessary noise and vibration throughout the boat.

A quick check of engine and shaft alignment is therefore a logical starting point in your relationship with a new engine. Keep in mind that the shaft may be precisely aligned when the boat is chocked up in the boatyard, but it may be a different story when the boat is floating in the water. No matter how well supported the hull is on dry land, it is only completely supported in the water, which can change shaft and engine alignment. Ideally, the installer or dealer should check the alignment after launching, but this is not always possible in the case of a new boat. Unless you're certain that someone has aligned the shaft properly after launching, however, the prudent owner will want to check this before starting the new engine and motoring away.

It's a quick job. Just loosen the four to six bolts of the shaft coupling, insert a feeler gauge between the plates (the actual thickness of the gauge chosen doesn't matter) and then retighten the bolts with light pressure. Next, leaving the feeler gauge in place, use another feeler gauge of the same thickness and check the opening between the faces of the shaft coupling at various spots around the coupling. If the engine is properly aligned, the spaces should be equal all around the shaft coupling. If the spaces show the same distance, remove the feeler gauge, and retighten the shaft coupling bolts. You can now use your engine with complete confidence in the alignment.

If there is more space at one point than another, adjustment of the engine mounting bolts (or a shifting of the engine laterally) by trial and error should quickly establish alignment. Once proper alignment is attained, make sure to retighten the engine mounting bolts before running the engine.

## Shaft Log Packing Nut

The shaft log packing nut is another item that can cause obscure problems. This is the large, double nut on the propeller shaft, just forward of the spot where the shaft enters through the boat's bottom or deadwood. It works like the packing gland on a household faucet. Flax packing material is wrapped around the shaft, and pressure on the nut compresses it to the point where the passage of water is blocked, without unduly interfering with the rotation of the shaft.

The traditional way to determine proper tightness for a shaft log packing nut is to count the number of drops of water per minute dripping off the nut (most experts say 3 to 6 drops per minute). The problem is, that the boat should be underway in order to get a proper reading with this method. If the boat has not yet been launched, there is a simple "backyard" method: Put the boat's transmission in neutral, and take hold of the propeller; it should turn with relatively light hand pressure. If it turns too easily, the nut should be tightened. If it requires too much pressure, back the nut off slightly.

If the boat is in the water, the same method can be used by placing a small pipe wrench on the shaft (forward of the nut) after wrapping the shaft with a piece of cloth or tape to prevent scarring. Again, relatively light pressure should rotate the shaft. A packing nut that is too loose will allow excessive amounts of water to enter the bilge; too tight will place undue strain on the engine and cause excessive wear on the shaft.

## Idle Speed

A high idle speed might have some good points in a car, where you have brakes. Unfortunately, in a boat, a high idle speed can cause problems when trying to maneuver in tight quarters, and tends to frazzle the nerves in docking situations. It's therefore a good idea to check the idle before setting out from the boatyard where you had your engine installed.

Carburetors on gas engines vary from model to model but the idle adjustment is easy to find. It is a screw with a spring tensioner surrounding it, that works against a stop that prevents the throttle control from being closed down to where the engine would stop. You can find the idle adjustment screw by working the throttle and seeing which level moves back and forth on the carburetor. At the end of this lever, you'll find the idle adjustment screw. (Diesel idle speed is set by adjusting the governor.)

You can't do any harm by turning this screw (although you can by turning the screw that adjusts the jets, so don't recklessly turn carburetor screws until you're sure that you have found the idle adjustment one.) When you do, turn it in the direction (usually, to the left) which will allow the throttle lever to close a little more toward the stop, causing the engine to slow somewhat. (Do this while the engine is warm and running.)

Once you have adjusted this screw to where it feels right for your usage, try pumping the throttle a few times to see where it settles at idle, then check the RPM. One or two slight changes in the screw setting will give you a proper idle speed.

## General

Now, with idle setting, alignment, and shaft log all properly adjusted, it's time to make a test run, but first make a final inspection of the engine room.

It's amazing what you might find, and you should at least come up with a couple of spare sockets or even a ratchet. Surely there will be an oily rag or two, and probably a box or two which once contained parts or accessories. Remove all the extraneous gear, and then look the engine over carefully. Are all lines and hoses connected? Are all wires attached at what appears to be logical spots? Are fuel, oil, and air filters in place?

This might seem to be a superfluous exercise, but anyone who has spent time in a boatyard knows well that mechanics are seldom (if ever) able to work uninterrupted on a single job. They are constantly called from one "emergency" situation to another, and two or three mechanics will often work on a job, each one assuming that someone else has performed the essential steps.

Now, if everything appears normal, it's time for a test run. The smartest way to test a new engine is the navy way, with the boat tied firmly to the dock. With bow and stern spring lines in place, start the engine and let it idle until it warms up. At this stage, keep your eyes glued to the temperature and oil pressure gauges. Building and assembling an engine requires a great amount of metal grinding. All loose flecks of metal should have been removed, but were they? Listen. If any unusual noises develop, shut the engine down immediately. If the temperature climbs above the operating temperature specified by the manufacturer, shut it down. If the oil pressure fails to climb quickly into the manufacturer's specified range, shut it down.

Now, try advancing the throttle a little. Don't overdo it, especially at first. Again check for unusual noises or unnatural changes in oil pressure or temperature. If all seems okay, let her run for a time at about 2000 or 2500 RPM. Is the temperature gauge settling down at a logical point?

With the engine back at idle speed again, try putting it in gear, both forward and reverse. Watch the tension on the dock lines to see if it's actually shifting. Don't pull the cleats out of the deck—just ease her back and forth a few times from neutral to forward, and from neutral to reverse.

If no problems are noted with the oil pressure and temperature, and none are experienced in testing the gearbox, it is reasonable to assume that you have a good engine and a good installation. Anything associated with the water, however, is best broken in carefully and approached with caution, at least until it's proven in use. Don't head off for Tahiti with a brand new engine, and don't run your new engine at full throttle for long periods until you are well past the manufacturer's specified break-in period. Change oil and oil filters at least as often as the manufacturer recommends; sooner, if you tend to run your engine for short periods only.

With a newly commissioned engine, this is a good time to make some resolutions with regard to operating under power. The greatest enemy of a marine engine is not overuse, it's lack of use, or running it for short periods when it never really reaches operating temperature. If you tend to use your engine only for leaving the slip or mooring, resolve to motor out to the harbor mouth from now on. Take occasional short cruises totally under power. You'll be rewarded with fewer repairs, and a longer engine life.

In all likelihood, with careful breaking in, you have years of trouble-free boating sitting in the engine room. But lemons do come off the best of production lines, and problems usually show up early in the life of a lemon. Therefore, plan a few shakedown trips close to home. Lengthen these as you build confidence in your new engine, treat it right, perform routine maintenance faithfully, and avoid dirty fuel.

## Diesel Engines

All of the above applies to diesels as well as gas engines (with the exception of the idle speed adjustment). For specifics on diesel idle speed adjustment for your particular diesel, check your owner's manual. The procedure will vary from engine to engine.

Some other differences between gas engines and diesels also deserve to be mentioned. Diesels of power ratings comparable to gas engines will appear to be larger and more rugged (which they usually are), but the fuel systems involves parts that are intricately machined. The tolerances in fuel pumps and injectors, for example, are extremely close, making them vulnerable to problems with fuel contaminated with extraneous debris or water. The source of your fuel and the condition of your tank should be considered carefully. When replacing a diesel engine, a new fuel tank might be a good investment. If you're switching engines from gas to diesel, a new tank might be a requirement.

Beyond this, be meticulous when it comes to checking and maintaining filters. Particular spots to watch are the primary and secondary fuel filters, and the strainer in the fuel lift pump.

Problems with diesels are few, but are sometimes difficult to diagnose. If your new engine should stop suddenly, consider that there might be an air lock in the fuel line. This could result from a fuel line that was disconnected when the engine was installed, or from a newly developed leak in the fuel system. Check your owner's manual for the procedure for bleeding the fuel line. It is generally straightforward and uncomplicated.

A air lock in the fuel line is the first thing to check for with a diesel that won't run, but there is another common problem that is more difficult to diagnose. Because they don't have an electrical ignition switch, some diesels employ an electric solenoid which shuts off the fuel flow. If the solenoid malfunctions, the fuel flow is cut off and the engine won't run. Troubleshoot this problem according to the owner's manual.

If a diesel engine runs poorly, lacks power, or shows a smoky exhaust, look first for problems with the exhaust system. Exhaust-system back pressure can show up as all sorts of apparent "engine" problems. Discuss this with your installer. It could be the answer to vague, hard-to-diagnose problems.

## OUTBOARD AUXILIARIES

Outboard auxiliaries are sometimes considered a poor man's answer to sailboat power, but in truth, today's outboards are incredibly reliable and trouble-free. A few comments should be made however, on commissioning the new outboard.

First, make sure you have a safety rope or chain on your outboard when you place it on the bracket or in the well. Generally, the installation of an outboard auxiliary is an awkward job, and one where a spot of oil on the cockpit sole can result in the engine resting on the bottom of the harbor, rather than on top of the transom. Resurrecting an engine that has been immersed in salt water can be an expensive (and not always satisfactory) job.

Next, make sure you tighten the bracket screws well, and check them from time to time for tightness. Vibration can fatigue or compress the fiberglass or wooden motor mount, so periodic retightening is good practice.

Install a good lock that covers both of the bracket clamps. A lock will not *guarantee* immunity from determined burglars, but burglars seem inclined toward choosing the easiest targets; your chances of keeping your outboard rise dramatically if it's locked to the boat.

And finally, as soon as you fire up your outboard, check that the cooling water bypass stream is spritzing with good volume. An overheated outboard can require expensive repairs, and this quick visual check should become a standard part of your outboard's every use.

As with all marine engines, outboards respond best to frequent and extended use. There has probably never been an outboard that has been worn out, but thousands have been underused to death. Given frequent use and careful maintenance, an outboard motor could outlast its owner.

# 6

# A Proper Name for a Proper Yacht

It might not have occurred to you that giving your boat a name is part of the commissioning process, but a proper yacht should not be launched until it is christened with the proper name it deserves. Therefore, now that we have dealt with some of the more serious and more objective aspects of commissioning, let's take a lighthearted look at the subject of boat names.

## NAMING YOUR BOAT

For the last decade or two our society has been obsessed with semantic overkill. How often do you hear a sentence that doesn't contain the words "really," "meaningful," "super," "high-technology," or "state-of-the-art"? And among our most obsessive conceits is the all-pervading matter of "making a statement." Today, we make a statement with everything we touch; from our after-shave lotion to the car we drive; and with our homes, clothes, magazine subscriptions and children's schools all huddled somewhere in between (and busy making statements of their own).

But there is an area where we do, legitimately, make a statement. In fact, the names we choose for our boats reveal much about our self-perceptions, our personalities, and our social attitudes.

Regrettably, boat naming is not without its fads, too. Twenty or thirty years ago, every other boat had a name comprised of the first syllables of the names of the owner's children. As this was

the post-war period when large families were in vogue, some boats found their transoms filled to the point where they looked like the backs of jerseys worn by Serbian football players. Boats with alphabet-soup names like *BarBoClairDawnSandy* littered anchorages all around the country.

The next period of excess saw a wild swing toward "cute" names, the archetype being the ubiquitous *Mama's Mink*. Although there were many variations on this theme, it's a sad commentary on the users' imagination that most adopted it intact, to the point where most harbors housed four or five *Mama's Mink*s. Most likely, these were owned by suburbanites who delighted in living in tract houses.

The next round of excess involved the addition of Roman numerals to the boat name; the larger the number, the greater the presumed wisdom and nautical experience of the owner. Fortunately, this tendency to boast of one's previous ownerships tended to die out as the numerals grew to ever more cumbersome proportions, with fewer and fewer observers capable of translating them from the Latin without assistance.

Finally, as our nation's boatowners struggled to break out of their group-think fixations, they moved toward names which they felt exhibited a greater sense of ambience (or ambivalence). Few were truly innovative thinkers, however; throughout this period almost every boat launched was named *Spindrift*, *Mistral*, or *Typhoon*.

But that's all history now. Where are we today? Happily, we do seem to be evolving into a state of maturity where our boats are carrying a wide spectrum of suitable and sibilant names that tend to evoke thoughts of what boating is really about. Oh... there are still excesses in evidence, but thankfully they are growing ever more rare with the passage of time.

Here, for the benefit of confused newcomers to the sport, and others who are faced with that gut-wrenching task of naming a new boat, we offer a few rules on boat naming:

1) There is no law requiring that boat names include some combination of "Sea," "See," or "C." Granted, there are times when the temptation is almost insurmountable. A Delaware optometrist who named his boat *Sea Swell* has not been ostracized by the local boating fraternity (and is even applauded by other optometrists).

The good Lord will surely forgive the person named Conrad or Childs, who having a wife and five children, can't resist painting *The Seven C's* on his stern. *SEAduction* and *SEAducer* are, however, indications of *InSEApeant SEArebral SEAnility*, and should be avoided.

2) Avoid names that can pique the curiosity of law enforcement officers. While *Gin 'n Tonic*, *Pot Barge*, or *Coke Float* might be reflections of your recreational proclivities, they do tend to

create long afternoons of conversation with uniformed visitors. He whose natural tendency is to taunt (or flaunt), will find more SEArenity on the water if he exercises a little more discretion.

**3)** The use of the owner's name spelled backwards lost legitimacy when Harry Conover's *Revenoc* was lost at sea. Hopefully, this aberration will not be revived. *Senoj, Htims,* or *Grebnettug* add little to the nautical scene, and can result in brain overload during the deciphering.

**4)** A boat's name need not make cryptic reference to its owner's occupation. There was a time when every dentist's boat was named *Trident* or *Flossum*, and every bookie's boat was named *You Bet!* Apparently, the sportfisherman's tendency to name his boat *Hooker* (or variations thereof) has lessened the sailor's compulsion to placard his (or his spouse's) occupation. Try to avoid this once-common error, unless you consider yourself some sort of SEAlebrity.

**5)** As a general rule, the owner's name is better left off the transom. This rule applies particularly to such miscarriages as *Jim Dandy, Andy's Candy* or *OffSHOR*. (One must, however, admit grudging admiration for the intrepid sailor with the temerity to name his sloop *Bermuda Shwartz*.)

A real life acquaintance with the family name of Seaward

showed admirable restraint when he refused to emblazon his signature across the stern, although he did fall short by using his grandchildren's names for sources. Fortunately, it was the dinghy that went through life with the lubberly *NickGeorge* on its nameboard, while his boat became *WenSam*. Certainly his initial restraint more than offsets this later fall from grace.

6) Multihulls do not require names that make reference to the fact that they have more than one hull. Names like *Cheshire Cat*, *Banana Split*, and *College Tri* are out. While *Double Dribble* may be appropriate for a leaky catamaran, it is a clear violation of rule number 4 if the owner plays for the NBA.

With the ground rules now defined, the question that should be addressed is: "Just how *does* one can come up with an outstanding boat name?" The answer, shipmates, lies in the owner's attitude toward his specific boat, and toward the subject of boating in general.

As a starting point, it should be observed that the name is the owner's personal property (not to mention his "statement"); thus he can range far in choosing (or coining) a name. French, Greek, or Polynesian words lend themselves well to this, and so do frank constructions that *sound* foreign. You could name your boat *Lacunai*, for example. It sounds vaguely like lagoon, which elicits visions of tropical anchorages. It has an "L" in it, which rolls nicely on the tongue, and it has a double "O" sound, which makes for a soothing and peaceful mood. When visitors ask its meaning you can just look mysterious, thus avoiding the admission that it is a medical term describing the areas of the pancreas which secretes insulin.

Go down to the harbor and take a moment or two to look around. Decide to adopt the third object your eyes fall on as your boat's name. If a *Kestrel*, a *Dolphin*, or a *Manatee* chance by, it's been a productive trip. If you chance to catch the *Johnny-on-the-Spot* out of the corner of your eye, return and repeat the procedure on another day.

Consider vague and cryptic references to your innermost feeling about boating. This can result in names ranging from *Tranquility* or *Repose*, to *Mal de Mer* or *Repulsion*. As an alternative, you could consider a name with a specific reference to the boat itself. You could paint your boat dark green, for example, and call it *Spinach*. If you are a firefighter, however, don't push this concept to the point of painting black spots on your boat and calling it *Dalmatian*.

Foreign, geographic references often have a nice sound and elicit pleasant associations, plus hinting at an impressive nautical background. *Finisterre* is probably the classic example of this genre, but you could adopt *Farallon*, *Good Hope*, or *Hebrides* without being accused of mimicry.

Coined words are absolutely acceptable, and don't have to have any real foundation, but make sure the name you choose is easily pronounceable. *Sibolette* or *Kestora* are quick examples, and don't have a bad ring to them. Feel free to use either if they should appeal to you.

And in conclusion, feel free to change the name of your boat if it does not appeal to you. We do not subscribe to the old superstition that it is bad luck to change the name of a boat. Rather, it may be that it is a source of bad luck to force a good boat to go through life with a bad name. If you find yourself in the position of new owner of *BobCarTedAl*, go ahead and change it.

## VINYL BOAT NAMES AND GRAPHICS

At one time a high art reserved for the specialist, applying the name to your boat's hull can now be done by almost anyone. You don't have to do it yourself, of course. You can still hire a sign painter, but the price of professional application may be several times higher, and the results are not necessarily guaranteed to be any better.

What many owners are doing is to hire a professional to prepare the boat name, including graphics, in the comfort of his workshop. Then the boatowner takes over and does the actual application himself.

The secret to the do-it-yourself application is a self-adhesive vinyl film—thin plastic sheets manufactured principally by 3M Company. The difference between these letters and the ones you buy for your mailbox is that the lettering and graphic designs come to you pre-arranged and pre-spaced on an application scrim—a see-through paper-like cloth.

For application, you clean the hull where the name will be placed (Windex is recommended for fiberglass), get the hull wet with a mild detergent and water solution, wet down the name and scrim, peel off the adhesive protector, then slap the letters and scrim onto the hull.

The detergent and water act as a lubricant, allowing you to slide, position, and reposition the boat name until you get it in the right spot. Once the name is positioned exactly right, you squeegee the detergent solution out, let everything dry, and peel off the application scrim. Whatever is vinyl—name and graphics—stays firmly attached. With incomplete squeegeeing, you may have some air bubbles which will need to be popped with a needle and forced down.

Once applied, the vinyl names seem to be long-lived, generally outlasting paint. Their abrasion resistance is about the same as paint, but the vinyl is resistant to deterioration by ultraviolet rays. These vinyl films have been in widespread use for more than ten years, and all the eight- to ten-year-old names we examined look almost as good as new.

Prices for the vinyl lettering itself vary a great deal. Material costs are minimal. If you want to cut and arrange letters yourself, you could probably buy leftover vinyl material from a big signmaker. The major cost comes in letter-cutting and design.

Looking for the best price on a boat name, we checked with the companies that advertise widely in boating magazines. We also checked our local yellow pages under "Signs" and discovered that 12 of the 17 sign companies listed were experienced in making the vinyl lettering and eager to quote us a price. We found that companies advertising "boat names" and "truck lettering" were generally well versed in making and applying the vinyl names.

From all the companies, we asked for quotes on both a plain letter name and a name with graphics.

## Plain Letter Names

For plain letter names, most of the price quotes were per letter, with considerable variation depending on style (typeface) and size. Since 4-inch letters are required for Coast Guard documentation, we got quotes on that size, the prices including spacing and alignment on the application scrim as well as the cutting of the letters.

Our best price came from one of the five local signmakers we checked with—a little over a dollar per letter for black letters and just slightly more for any of a dozen other colors. This signmaker offered a choice of nine stock typefaces, which are cut by a machine. As the price goes up, so does the range of choices of type style and color.

Such standard lettering appears to be a competitive market. The highest local quote we got for plain lettering was less than two dollars per letter. If we had preferred one of the styles from that signmaker, the price difference probably wouldn't have been significant.

Of the companies that advertise nationally, only one was in the same ball park as the locals; the other national companies were considerably higher. We concluded that for plain lettering, your best bet is likely to be a local signmaker.

## Custom Lettering

If you are interested in anything other than plain lettering, your shopping will be considerably more complicated. All the local signmakers we checked had a limited supply of typefaces. Nevertheless, if you don't find one you like in their catalogs, you can generally special order one.

Locally, we found that we could order any type style that a commercial typesetter could generate, literally hundreds of variations. A typesetter produces the name, usually on photographic paper, then the signmaker transfers the name to the standard 3M vinyl. You pay for the extra cost of typesetting, plus the hand cutting by the signmaker; prices will vary considerably. Generally you can expect the cost to be about triple that of standard machine-cut letters, perhaps more if the signmaker or typesetter is doing some design work in the process.

The high price of custom work from the local signmakers may make a turn to one of the national companies more attractive, since they all have a broader selection of styles. One, for example, has 46 different lettering styles and 26 colors to choose from. To decide if any of these are better for you, there is really no shortcut to ordering the catalogs and examining the sample type styles.

## Custom Designs

If you want something more elaborate than a plain name (personalized or multicolor lettering, hull graphics, a customized logo or special design work) the cost escalates rapidly.

The national companies all have a supply of stock symbols and graphics that they can incorporate into the lettering for simple application. It's an odd assortment—flowers, beer mugs, dice, anchors, eagles, unicorns, Vikings, mermaids, kangaroos, hearts, or shamrocks—but the cost is low enough to make the option attractive. Typically, a stock graphic can be incorporated for the cost of two or three letters. Custom design work is a whole different ball game.

Locally, almost all signmakers will do custom graphics; however, most of them are not really artists (some of them don't realize this). On the other hand, the signmakers we talked to all appeared to be good craftsmen, and they could convert almost any artistic design into a vinyl name. You will pay for their time and craftsmanship, and the wise buyer will also pay for an artist to execute the design for the signmaker to follow.

For serious custom designing, the nationally advertised boat namers are again worth considering. Together, the three companies we talked to probably have more experience at boat work than all the local shops combined, and consequently have a better sense of what is going on in boat graphics and what needs to be done.

For example, we spent a frustrating half-hour trying to explain to a local commercial artist everything about a potential graphic, from the need for four-inch letters to the complexities of the sheerline and the compound curves of our hull and transom. We wanted the graphic to lean toward the rear on both sides—right on the starboard and left on the port side. We're not at all sure she understood the requirements of boat lettering, and we didn't want to pay for her education (and maybe mistakes) in the field, especially since we couldn't get a firm quote on the maximum price.

For the national companies, the costs are again open-ended, depending on what you want, but the companies seem to be fairly straightforward about the matter. Prism, for example, says "Complexity varies, so exact costs can't be determined until the design is established. As a guideline, the average cost of one completed graphic is $175 to $225 which includes a $100 design fee." They require a non-refundable $100 deposit with an order for a custom graphic. On-The-Hull says, "Custom orders will be priced individually. Prepayment is required only after you have accepted our price."

We did not pursue a custom design through to completion with both a local and a national company, but the figures cited by the national companies seemed reasonable to us—about the same as from our local signmakers.

One other note about custom work: once the design is done, there should be only a small additional charge for a reproducible copy of the art; that is, a copy of the name graphic done at small scale that can then be reproduced on T-shirts, glasses, stationery, or other personalized nautical accessories.

In summary, for complex or custom work, the major part of what you're buying is artistry or design—at fees which are anything but fixed or easily quoted. If you know a local designer or artist and have confidence in his or her work, consider having a local signmaker execute the artist's design in vinyl. Otherwise, you should consider one of the national companies with more experience in boat work.

# Volume II • Part Two:
# Seasonal Commissioning And Decommissioning

# 7

# Winter Layup and Storage

## THE SEASON'S END

As the frost line marches southward in October and November, it signals the end of the season for sailors "stranded" to its north. The end of the sailing season, however, doesn't mean the end of a boatowner's responsibilities; owning a boat is a year-round proposition. A pleasure for some, a chore for others, off-season layup and winter's armchair sailing is all part of the game.

In a way, if you use your boat for only half a year, it might be a plus. If you have ever looked at a boat that has been in the Caribbean charter trade for a few years, you realize that the concept of the no-maintenance fiberglass boat is something of a myth. Winter layup provides an opportunity for boats and boatowners to rest and regroup, and a chance to keep up or catch up with ongoing maintenance tasks.

The time to begin off-season projects is in the fall, not in the spring. Over the winter months, if you can at least make notes about what needs to be done, and line up the required tools and supplies, you'll have a jump on recommissioning in the spring. If you can complete some of the items on that list in the fall or over the winter, you won't find yourself still on the "hard" when others are enjoying the first warm weekends of the new season.

### Wet or Dry Storage?

If you own a boat built of fiberglass, aluminum, or steel, it's going to last longer if stored out of the water when not in use. Although the mechanics of gelcoat blistering are not fully understood, there does appear to be a definite relationship between the amount of time the boat spends in the water and the likelihood of gelcoat blistering. That doesn't mean that if you haul the boat out every time you use it you won't get blisters. It simply means that all other things being equal, a fiberglass boat in the water is more likely to blister than a boat ashore.

Corrosion is the problem with aluminum and steel boats stored in salt water. In many marinas, poor wiring—either that of the marina or that of boats docked there—puts a lot of electrical current into the water, accelerating the natural tendency of these materials to corrode. The problems caused by stray current in the water may even be worse in the winter months due to the use of various types of electric-powered systems to prevent icing in the wet storage area of the marina or boatyard. In fresh water free of pollutants and electrical currents, the corrosion of steel and aluminum is minimized. But these conditions are rare indeed.

Carvel-planked wooden boats, on the other hand, almost always fare better when stored in the water. Although the metal in a wooden boat (fastenings, through-hull fittings, props) will be more likely to corrode when the boat is in the water, a more important consideration is the stability of a wooden boat's structure by keeping the moisture content of the wood as constant as possible year round.

Cold-molded wooden boats which are theoretically free from the problems of moisture stabilization, are the exception. Their epoxy coating, if undamaged, is highly resistant to the penetration of water. An epoxy-sheathed wooden boat is best stored out of the water, to avoid damage to the sheath which could allow water to enter the wood.

If you store a boat in the water, be prepared to pay at least the same amount you would for storing the boat on land. For the marina operator, wet storage is almost always more of a headache than a boat stored ashore. Lines chafe and stretch, fenders chafe on topsides, boats leak and sometimes sink, untended by owners who are busy elsewhere. Wet storing a boat is a serious responsibility for both the marina operator and the owner. If you can't realistically expect to check your boat in the water once a week, it is essential that you come to terms with the marina or boatyard with regard to their degree of responsibility. These terms should be spelled out in the contract, with the charges for various services detailed.

## Hauling Out

There are, of course, risks entailed every time you haul a boat. Boats are occasionally damaged in every form of lifting and hauling—trailers, cranes, mobile lifts, and railways. It is best to stay completely away from your boat while it is being hauled. If it is damaged, you want to be certain that the responsibility for the damage lies with the person hauling the boat. It is extremely rare that a boatowner will be more knowledgeable than the marina operators about how a boat should be hauled. If you have any doubt about the competence of the yard, watch how they haul other boats before committing your boat into their hands.

Immediately after your boat is hauled, the bottom should be scrubbed. Marine growth gets more tenacious if it is allowed to dry before you try to remove it. Usually, the boatyard will wash the bottom of the boat with a high-pressure hose for a fee based on the overall length. It's almost always worth the extra cost.

If at all possible, you should look at the bottom of your boat before it is washed to determine the effectiveness of your bottom paint. Once it's clean, you'll never know how good your $125 per gallon paint really is.

## Covered or Uncovered?

The question of whether a boat should be covered if stored outside in a northern climate is a matter of some debate, although most experts agree that any boat in dry storage should be covered (but well ventilated) regardless of the climate. Woven polyethylene tarps are relatively durable and inexpensive, and framing materials such as PVC pipe and electrical conduit are cheap and easy to work with. Yard rates for inside storage is affordable for some, but paying yard labor rates to build a fancy wooden framework or paying a sailmaker to make a custom canvas boat cover seems unnecessarily extravagant.

Water can make its way into the tiniest cracks and crevices where it becomes absorbed by the laminate or wood structure. If that water freezes and expands, there is even more chance for damage. Moreover, air pollution being what it is, an uncovered boat becomes stained with grit and grime that can be difficult to remove. The combined effects of a winter's worth of ice, snow, and ultraviolet light can make recommissioning in the spring that much more tedious if a boat is left uncovered.

Later in this chapter, we'll discuss the construction of an inexpensive, reusable framework and cover that will help protect a boat during off-season storage.

## Cradle or Jackstands?

One of the marine industry's greatest inventions for speeding up the hauling and layup process is the screw-type jackstand. Before jackstands, the crane or mobile lift might be tied up for an hour supporting a boat while wooden poppets were fitted to the hull, with their accompanying system of diagonal supports, longitudinals, and heavy base timbers. On a 40-footer, this might take two men an hour. The same job can be done with four jackstands in ten minutes by one man, and if properly done, will support the boat just as well or better.

A boat dealer will undoubtedly encourage you to purchase a cradle with a new boat (and why shouldn't he?), but a custom-fitted cradle is of no particular advantage as far as most boatyards are concerned. A cradle is heavy and takes up a lot of space, and will only fit your boat or another just like it. A jackstand can be carried by one man, while a cradle may have to be dragged around by a tractor. It all costs time and money.

While no boatyard goes out of its way to improperly store a boat, it pays for you to cast a weather eye on the way your boat is chocked up. Whether sailboat or powerboat, the keel should be supported by heavy timbers to help distribute the load on the ground. On soft ground, this will help keep the boat from settling into the ground, redistributing the loads on the hull.

Jackstands aren't foolproof. Each leg of the stand should be backed up by a foot pad to keep the legs from sinking into the ground. The best pad is a piece of 3/4-inch plywood, large enough to really distribute the load.

The screw pads of the jackstands should be tightened up firmly against the hull, but they should not distort it in any way. Fin keel boats with flat bilges are the boats most at risk in this respect. Frequently, the hull structure is strong enough to support the keel with the boat in the water, but the weight of the boat on the keel ashore is sometimes enough to distort the hull. To overcome this problem, the tendency is to overtighten the jackstands to take more of the weight off the keel, which usually only compounds the distortion problem. The answer is usually to use more than the normal four jackstands so that more of the load can be removed from the keel without localizing the stress in a few areas of the hull. Be prepared to pay extra for the use of the additional jackstands.

The angle of the stand to the hull is also important. Although the heads of jackstands are equipped with ball joints to allow the plywood support pads to swivel, you should try to position the stands so that the load on them is as close to pure compression as possible. This will reduce the tendency of the stands to be forced out away from the hull as load is applied to them. On powerboats, this is usually easy. On sailboats, it can require some juggling of the stands to get the best angle.

On sailboats, the jackstands should be located as far outboard from the center of the boat as is practical. This will help to stabilize the boat in high winds.

### The Mast In or Out?

Whether the boat is stored in or out of the water, the choice between leaving the mast stepped or unstepped is seldom an easy one. The decision is usually left to the boatowner unless the boatyard requires the mast be unstepped or, conversely, doesn't have the equipment to pull the stick. Given a choice, this question is commonly answered on the basis of cost; it's cheaper to leave it stepped—or at least it seems so.

Perhaps the decision is difficult because the question has no firm answer, just a host of considerations that the boatowner must face before making his decision. In addition to the cost of pulling the mast, some of those considerations are:

• Are weather conditions, notably wind strength and direction, such that the windage of a stepped mast can topple the boat from her cradle or poppets or put undue strain on docklines?

• Does the marina or boatyard have the equipment, personnel, and experience to give reasonable assurance that unstepping and restepping the mast can be done without damage?

• A mast should be carefully inspected from end to end annually. Is a slow trip up the mast in a boatswain's chair feasible, or would that inspection be done better with the mast laid horizontally a few feet from the ground?

• Can the boat be adequately covered with the mast in place? Can the rigging be tied off or replaced by messenger lines so they do not abrade themselves or the spars?

• If the mast is unstepped, will it be stored out of the elements in a safe place? Does the price of unstepping include storage in a weatherproof mast shed, or will it simply be placed on an outdoor rack?

For storage in areas with even moderately severe winter weather conditions, we tend to favor the removal of spars during the off-season. With a wooden mast, removal is almost mandatory for maintenance and painting or varnishing. Another instance where removal is particularly helpful is with aluminum spars that are painted, as touching up dings and bare spots is far easier with the mast out. Even with anodized aluminum spars, a seamanlike compulsion to know what sort of wear and corrosion is taking place aloft often dictates that the mast be stepped and unstepped annually.

The cost of unstepping the mast runs several dollars per foot, but usually includes restepping and rerigging. It's a good idea to be on hand when the mast is pulled, in part to ensure that the spars are being handled properly, but mostly because it provides an opportunity to inspect the rig and to discover items needing repair. Once the mast is stored safely in the mast shed, cover it loosely with an old tarp or a sheet of polyethylene to help keep it clean over the winter.

Is the cost of annual stepping and unstepping worth it? Apparently not if ninety percent of the boats stored in the typical boatyard is any indication. The cacophony of slapping halyards in most winter storage yards is evidence enough to prove that most boatowners choose to leave their spars stepped.

It's quite likely that the wear on a stepped mast and its rigging (and the possibilities for damage) are just as great in the off-season as during a season of sailing. And, of course, wear (and damage) always end up costing money. Perhaps worse, a rigging failure could result in the loss of the use of the boat while it awaits a new mast or piece of rigging.

When one thinks of the ice crystals inside swaged terminals, aluminum oxidizing under the mast boot, thimbles worn to paper-thinness, and a host of other possible sources of damage, some real and some imagined; the cost of taking the mast out seems quite reasonable.

## Some Tips on "Dry Storing" a Mast

There is little to be gained from taking a mast out of a boat and leaving it lying just anywhere unprotected and unchecked. If you do take the mast out, do the job right and take advantage of the fact that it's in a position to be worked on, and then store it where weather and accidents can do it no harm.

First detach the spreaders where they attach to the mast. You may even want to remove the upper shrouds with the spreaders and store them separately to make a more compact package of the mast. Disconnect and detach masthead instruments to reduce the chance of damage.

Go over the whole rig carefully from top to bottom. Obviously, it is better to find problems with plenty of time to correct them than on the eve of restepping. Check for cracks, worn clevis pins, broken cotter pins, corrosion under tangs (a grayish powder and roughness at their edges), elongated sheave bearings or worn pins, chewed sheave grooves and exit boxes, and dings or dents in the luff groove or sailtrack. Remove the mast boot and plastic spreader-tip covers (the most likely places for corrosion).

If halyards or fittings need replacement, take them off to use as a model. If halyards and stays are replaced while they still have use in them, they can still be used as spares. Run a soft rag down all wire rigging; a broken strand should catch a thread and give itself away. Inspect all terminal fittings for cracks or corrosion. Then thoroughly wash the spar and rigging. This is especially important if the boat is kept in salt water or near sources of industrial pollution. Use a liquid detergent and fresh water under pressure.

Tie the rigging securely to the mast, then wrap the whole rig loosely in polyethylene or canvas (old boat covers work well as do household tarpaulins cut into strips). Leave the ends of the cover open for ventilation.

In the spring, lubricate everything that moves, touch up nicks (epoxy is good for polyurethane-coated spars), and rewash the rig (to keep the sails from being stained).

*    *    *

Try not to make decommissioning a chore. It certainly is not a time any sailor regards as a pleasure, but it need not be a hassle either. Instead, make an hour spent at haul-out worth two hours at outfitting time. Not only will the time saved make the real chore of outfitting easier to bear, but it will provide a sense of accomplishment to hopefully last through the off-season.

## A LAYUP CHECKLIST

___ Ensure that the weight of the boat is solidly on the keel, and that poppets or jackstands do not deflect hull.

___ Clean the boat bottom. Make sure that it is free of oil and other fouling.

___ Wax gelcoat; touch up paint.

___ Drain water from tanks, seacocks, mufflers, heat exchangers, hot water heaters, and other plumbing.

___ Inspect fuel system for leaks. Fill diesel fuel tanks; empty or top off gasoline tanks per requirements of boatyard.

___ Tie off running rigging or replace with messenger lines, and slacken standing rigging slightly, if the mast is left stepped. Cover mast and store indoors if unstepped.

___ Lubricate all fittings with moveable parts.

___ Cover or remove vulnerable equipment such as life rafts, outboard motors, tools, winches, windvanes, solar chargers, compasses and cockpit-mounted instruments.

___ Winterize engine per manufacturer's instructions.

___ Remove batteries, recharge, and store indoors.

___ Remove food and beverages, fabric and paper items (including books and charts).

___ Clean all lockers and drawers; leave open.

___ Clean bilge and allow to dry. Leave interior access hatches open, limber holes free of debris, and drain plug removed.

___ Empty and clean icebox; leave open.

___ Empty or remove stove fuel tank(s).

___ Clean stove and oven; coat with rust inhibitor; leave burner valves open.

___ Wash, dry, and coil all lines and rodes.

___ Update list of repairs and list of materials and supplies needed for recommissioning.

___ Wash and dry all interior surfaces and inside lockers to prevent mold and mildew.

___ Flush marine toilets and pump dry or fill with antifreeze per manufacturer's recommendations.

___ Remove all sails; fold and bag; take to sailmaker for cleaning and repair if necessary.

___ Decommission the dinghy and store indoors if possible.

___ Inventory all equipment removed from boat and note where it will be stored.

___ Erect frame and install cover.

___ Notify your insurance company that the boat has been hauled and is out of commission.

## WINTERIZING THE ENGINE

Winterizing an inboard engine installation means a lot more than filling the cooling system with antifreeze and stuffing a rag in the exhaust outlet. It means tending to needs of the exhaust system, the fuel system, the engine controls, and other components of the drive train, such as the shaft and prop. If you want to do these jobs yourself, plan on a long day of work, or perhaps a leisurely weekend.

Winterizing an engine can be time consuming, but none of the individual jobs are difficult. Doing the work yourself will pay off both in dollars and in an improved understanding of your boat's propulsion system. At thirty or forty dollars per hour, the simple projects described here can save you hundreds of dollars each season. Few special tools are required, and no advanced mechanic's skills are necessary.

While many items of drive-train maintenance can be done as easily in the spring as in the fall, the rush to get the boat back in commission frequently means that some items fall to the bottom of the priority list, and may never get done. With a properly winterized engine, however, most of the maintenance required prior to launching will already have been done when spring rolls around again.

There are sailors who neglect their boats' mechanical components with the attitude that sailors don't really need to know such things. Often, these auxiliaries die with less than a thousand hours on them, or their gearboxes or shift linkages fail just when the owner is attempting a difficult docking maneuver.

(When would you guess that a shift linkage would seize? Certainly not when you are traveling in a straight line at six knots.)

## Fuel System

The first component of the drive system to be attended to is the fuel system. Whether you have a diesel engine or a gas engine, a fuel additive can be used to stabilize the fuel during the storage period, even if it is only a month or two. Diesel and gasoline stabilizers are not interchangeable. Diesel fuel additives usually have biocides to prevent the growth of system-clogging organisms in the fuel.

As obvious as it may sound, read the instructions before buying a fuel stabilizer. Some require draining the tank before treatment, others require adding fuel to the tank after treatment, and some can just be poured into a full tank. In any case, it is important to run the engine for a few minutes after treating the fuel, so that the additive gets into the fuel lines and filters, and into the carburetor of a gas engine or the injectors of a diesel.

If the boat is already on land when you go through the winterizing process, run a garden hose to the raw-water intake to provide engine cooling water. Most engine intakes are smaller than the plastic or metal end fitting on a garden hose. A short length of tubing with a female fitting on one end can simply be screwed onto the hose, and the other end jammed into the raw-water intake. Someone should keep an eye on the hose while the engine is running just to make sure it does not pop out. Another way to do this is to remove the intake hose from the seacock, and place the hose in a bucket of water. Then use the garden hose to replace the water in the bucket that is sucked up into the engine.

Fuel filters can also be changed at this time. A strainer-type gasoline filter should be cleaned with fresh gasoline (not on board the boat) to remove sediment, and the bowl of the filter should be drained. Likewise, it is also important to drain the water from a diesel fuel separator, particularly on a boat stored in a cold climate. If fuel filter elements are changed before treating the fuel, they will become filled with stabilized fuel when the engine is run.

There are two schools of thought about storing fuel in the tanks when the boat is laid up. In the past, with gasoline systems using copper tanks and copper fuel lines, the practice was usually to drain the system to prevent the formation of "gum" or "varnish." With modern gasoline and stabilizers, this problem is minimized, and tanks should fare well if left full.

Opinion about the condition of diesel fuel tanks during layup varies. It is true that during layup, suspended sediment in diesel fuel will settle out on the bottom of the tank. This sediment could perhaps be a problem next season, if you were sailing in very rough conditions with very little fuel in the tank. The sediment could be stirred up, resulting in badly contaminated fuel. That, of course, is why you should have two filters in your diesel fuel system.

At the same time, an empty or half-full metal fuel tank in a boat laid up in cold climate can generate a lot of condensation. If you have a black iron diesel fuel tank, the condensation can accelerate corrosion. The safest course is to keep the fuel tank full on any boat having metal tanks.

Fiberglass tanks present another set of problems. Although the typical orthophthalic resin used in boatbuilding is highly resistant to chemicals, it is not perfectly resistant. Isophthalic resins offer considerably more resistance to attack by chemicals and solvents, and are therefore preferable for use in fuel tanks. Until recently, however, relatively few builders have used iso-phthalic resins because of the additional cost. If you have fiber-glass fuel tanks, and are unsure of the resin used in their construction, it would be prudent to lay up the boat with the tanks empty.

## Engine
Change the oil in the crankcase with the engine still warm from running treated fuel through the system. Unless your engine has a built-in crankcase pump, in most cases you will have to pump the oil out through the dipstick hole. You can either use a manual pump, or any one of a number of small impeller pumps designed to fit in the chuck of a 1/4-inch drill. The drill-driven pumps are quicker, and are frequently easier to use in the crowded engine compartment. Some of them, however, use a rubber impeller which is not designed to run dry, so that they can have a short life if the pump does not prime quickly.

After draining the oil, change the oil filter if the engine is equipped with a spin-on filter; then fill the engine with fresh oil. It is particularly important to change the oil when laying up a diesel engine. Most diesel fuel contains sulfur in varying amounts. A byproduct of the combustion of diesel fuel which contains sulfur is sulfuric acid which, over time, can cause serious engine problems.

If your transmission is lubricated separately from the engine, check the fluid at least twice a year, or more often on a boat whose engine gets frequent or extended use. It's impossible to change engine oil and gear lube too frequently.

The engine's cooling system must also be winterized. With a fresh-water-cooled engine, check the fluid level in the coolant tank, topping up with a 1:1 mixture of water and antifreeze if necessary. The next step is basically the same for both raw-water-cooled and fresh-water-cooled engines. The raw cooling water must be replaced with an antifreeze mixture. Dip the water inlet hose into a bucket of antifreeze. Now a little coordination is required. You want to start the engine and run it long enough to make sure that the antifreeze mixture has filled the cooling system, including the muffler. You will know you have done this when the cooling water ejected through the exhaust is the color of the antifreeze mixture.

At the same time, you don't want to run the engine after you've sucked up the entire bucket of antifreeze. You want the raw-water system to be full of antifreeze, not empty. It will take two people; one to hold the hose in the bucket, and one to operate the engine and watch the exhaust. Obviously, a positive means of communication between the two persons involved is also required. Over the noise of the engine, your voice may not travel to the helm from belowdecks (even though it's guaranteed to travel across the boatyard).

Don't try to save time by running the engine only once to circulate treated fuel, to heat up the oil for changing, and to suck up the antifreeze. You probably need about ten minutes of engine running for winterizing the fuel system and warming up the oil. Sucking up the antifreeze will only take a minute or less.

A gallon of antifreeze (two gallons of 1:1 mix) should handle engines up to about 40 horsepower. Then add extra for the hoses.

The length of run of the raw-water discharge hose to the muffler is as much a determinant of the amount of antifreeze used as is the size of the engine.

After shutting down the winterized engine, remove the ignition key and spray the inside of the switch with a lubricant like WD-40 or CRC.

## Exhaust System

If you have pumped enough antifreeze through your engine so that the discharged cooling water looks exactly like the antifreeze mixture in the bucket, the waterlift muffler should now be well protected. If you want to be extra cautious, install a drain plug in the muffler and drain it when laying up the engine. Reinstall the plug immediately after draining so you don't have to worry about replacing it in the spring. The same goes for any other drain plugs in the system that you remove. Reinstall them now, not later.

## Shaft and Prop

Haul-out time is the proper time to check the condition of the prop, shaft, cutlass bearing, and stuffing box. On a boat that is laid up ashore for the winter months, you can save yourself a fair amount of effort in the spring by doing these tasks when your other drive system layup is done.

First, check the prop for damage and corrosion. Pitting of the blades or discoloration may indicate an electrolysis problem which should be tracked down over the winter.

Wiggle the prop shaft in the cutlass bearing. There should be no slop, only the yielding of the rubber against the metal shaft. If the rubber bearing is worn, get a replacement now, rather than waiting until spring. Cutlass bearing replacement has the nasty habit of becoming a real project, as the bearing shell frequently seizes in the strut, and must be sawn out or punched out.

This is also a good time to check the shaft for wear. Disconnect the shaft flange at the transmission, and pull the shaft out far enough to see the surface of the shaft where it normally sits in the stuffing box and cutlass bearing. A shaft which is worn at the stuffing box may be very hard to seal. Tightening the stuffing box to overcome leaking around a worn shaft will only aggravate the problem. Winter is the time to deal with these projects, rather than the spring, when your primary concern is getting the boat back in commission.

If you have a folding prop, check the blades for slop at the pivot pin. Unless the pin fit is tight, wear will increase, not only in the prop blades, but at the cutlass bearing and stuffing box as well. A machine shop can bush the hole in the blades for the pivot pin, restoring a tight fit, and you can easily replace the pin if necessary. If you try to get this done in the spring, you may find everyone too busy to help you.

Don't try to check the engine and shaft alignment with the boat out of the water. This is particularly true with a flat-bottomed, fin-keeled boat. The weight of the hull on the keel can easily affect the engine alignment. In fact, if you have a fin keel with the engine sitting in the middle of the boat, it's not a bad idea to disconnect the shaft before the boat is hauled, to minimize the possibility of damage if the hull should flex. Later, after the boat is hauled and chocked up, any misalignment between the flange on the gearbox and the flange on the shaft will serve as an indicator of distortion in the hull.

## Engine Controls

On a boat used in salt water, there is a good chance that the shift and throttle controls have ingested a fair amount of salt over the course of the season. You may want to disassemble the control levers, clean them with fresh water, and give them a dose of spray lubricant.

This is particularly true with controls using pot metal or aluminum components. A surprising number of engine controls use galvanically incompatible materials which turn to powder in a few years of use in salt water if cleaning and lubricating are not done regularly.

On controls mounted in the cockpit well, check the back side of the mechanism to make sure that it is still well greased.

\* \* \*

It takes a fair amount of self-discipline to tackle the jobs associated with laying up an engine system, particularly when your primary interest is in putting the boat away for a while—not fussing with it. Nevertheless, this is true preventive maintenance; it will pay off with reduced maintenance costs and more reliable operation of the drive system, as well as giving you a headstart on the next sailing season.

Performing your own engine layup will give you more practical knowledge about the operation of the mechanical systems than a lifetime of turning the key and pushing the levers. Doing it yourself can not only save you money, but it can help you spot potential problems before they interrupt your next sailing season.

# STORING YOUR BOAT AT HOME

If you plan to tackle an extensive list of winter boat projects, if the drive from home to the boatyard takes up a good deal of your available work hours, and if you have a large yard or driveway (and understanding neighbors); this might be the year that you consider taking your boat home for the winter.

Until recently, it was impractical to transport any boat larger than a "trailerable" one home for the winter. If you did not own a trailer, you had to hire a boat mover and you needed a cradle strong enough to be jacked off the trailer in the backyard. Times have changed, however.

Two modern developments have made it both physically and financially practical to take boats of almost any size home for the winter: one is the hydraulic boat trailer, and the other is the adjustable jackstand. Hydraulic trailers come in various configurations; some are quite elaborate and capable of moving very heavy boats of 50 or 60 feet LOA—not exactly what you would consider trailerable. Some of these trailers are even submersible and do not require that the boat be hauled with a mobile lift. If a launching ramp is available with sufficient water over it, the trailer can be winched down into the water and the boat floated over it.

Hydraulic arms and pads on these trailers make cradles superfluous. Like the arms of giant robots, the supports are maneuvered under and against the boat while it is on the trailer, supporting as little or as much of the weight of the boat as is considered necessary. Once in your backyard or driveway, blocking is put under the open center of the trailer, and the boat is gently lowered onto it by dropping the entire trailer bed with built-in hydraulic cylinders. Screw jackstands are then placed under the boat, and the trailer pulled free. An experienced operator can load or unload a boat in a matter of minutes.

It is rare that you can actually store the boat at home more cheaply than you can in a boatyard, unless you have your own trailer. Usually, the total cost of hauling, launching, and trucking back and forth comes to about the same as winter storage at the boatyard. If you have a lot of work to do on the boat over the winter, however, taking the boat home can be an excellent idea. It's a lot easier to go out and putter on the boat for a few hours in the evening or on the weekend if it's sitting in the driveway or the backyard.

If you are going to store your boat at home, you will have to make sure that there is room to back the truck into your storage spot, and that the place you've picked to store the boat is firm enough to support both the weight of the boat and the weight of the tractor and trailer. Don't try to move the boat onto grass shortly after a heavy rain, as the truck may bog down.

Whether you're storing the boat on an asphalt driveway or on grass, make sure there are large, thick plywood pads under each leg of each support, and that there is good, load-distributing blocking under the keel. Few blacktop driveways are designed for the heavy loads that will be put on them by a big boat. You may park your car there with no problem, but your car is relatively light and probably moved to a slightly different spot every day, minimizing the "creep" of the blacktop. Your boat, on the other hand, may not move for months and may slowly sink into the surface; you must tend the boat supports periodically to make sure that the hull is not unevenly loaded.

You should also check the route home for low overpasses, low powerlines, and overhanging trees. Even a small tree branch can scratch through the paint or gelcoat on the boat's topsides. Varnished trim on deck can be covered with plastic film or old blankets to protect it. You can also drape the front of the boat with blankets or and old tarp to minimize the risk of nicks and scratches on the topsides. Don't forget power lines in your

*The modern hydraulic trailer has made it practical to take even large boats home for the winter. This boat, on its way to the owner's backyard, is almost fifty feet long and weighs over 26,000 pounds.*

driveway or yard, too. Every year, a number of sailors are electrocuted when they touch power lines, usually while launching boats or stepping masts.

There is also the matter of zoning regulations. Be sure you are on firm legal footing before dropping the boat in the yard. It could be very expensive to have to move it in the middle of winter if a neighbor complains. The responsibility for saying yea or nay to backyard boat storage rests with different authorities in different towns. One boatowner complained that he spent the better part of the day on the telephone being shuffled from the planning commission to the city solicitor to the city zoning board in order to put his 47-footer in the backyard. When he finally got approval, it was unclear whether that approval carried any legal weight, or if it was just an anonymous city employee giving an off-the-cuff judgment. When you get approval, get the name of the person giving you permission.

There is a risk of damage to your boat while it is being moved, but that can be minimized with careful planning and preparation. If you are only moving your boat a few miles on city streets at a very low speed, the preparation for moving is a lot less elaborate than if you are moving it fifty miles over the highway. In town, the trucker is not likely to travel at more than 15 miles an hour, and fairly loosely secured protective covers will survive. On the highway, they would be torn to ribbons, probably doing more harm than good in the process.

Here's a list for preparing your boat for highway transport, provided by the boat hauling division of Kenosha Auto Transport (202 Greenfield Rd., Lancaster, PA 17601). The requirements below are for over-the-road hauling and are far more stringent than for a simple move around town, but they provide conservative guidelines for any type of boat moving, including trailering with your own trailer.

• All items inside the boat, such as galley utensils, plates, cups, and bottles, should be properly secured. Better yet, take them off the boat.

• If mounted in a way that exposes them to damage, equipment such as radios, depthsounders, compasses, and knotmeters should be removed and stored inside.

• To prevent wind damage, canvas items such as awnings, Bimini tops, and dodgers should be removed prior to shipment.

• Ports, hatches, and windows should be dogged down tightly, and the locking device taped over to keep it from vibrating loose.

• Cabinet doors, drawers, and all lockers inside the boat must be secured in the closed position.

• Plastic or plexiglass windshields should be covered or removed and stored inside, as they are easily scratched.

It's also a good idea to drain your water tanks before moving the boat. This will not only make the boat lighter, but will prevent possible damage to the tank from surging liquid. Draining the fuel would be a good idea, but this is usually less practical.

If you are taking your spars home, all rigging should be lashed firmly to the mast, or removed. Rigging can easily chafe through the paint, varnish, or anodizing on a mast. If you have not already done it, remove any antennas or instrumentation from the top of the mast. You can store your spars at home on sawhorses or concrete blocks. Whichever you choose, you must shim the tops of the supports so that the mast is secured in place without drooping. The advantages of concrete-block supports are that they are cheap, and you can shim the mast level by slipping pieces of plywood between the mast and the blocking. In the spring, your can raise the mast to a comfortable working height by adding one or two blocks to each stack.

Don't forget to cover the mast with a tarp. You can also use clear polyethylene sheeting for an aluminum mast. Don't use it for a wooden mast, for the greenhouse effect of the sun on the plastic can wreak havoc on a varnished surface.

If you have a lot of work in front of you, taking your boat home can be a significant help in getting it done. As you gaze at the boat through the kitchen window over your morning coffee, your eyes may develop a permanent far away stare, but we guarantee you will never be bored.

# A PROPER WINTER COVER

If you've been getting by for years on makeshift covers—perhaps an old sail draped over a spar lashed to the deck—it's time to consider doing it right. A good winter cover and frame will simplify the task of layup, protect the boat, even make winter and early spring maintenance tasks easier.

The heart of a winter cover is the frame that supports it. Good frames can be built from wood, from steel electrical conduit, or from PVC pipe and plumbing fittings. Which you choose is more a matter of inclination than any real difference in quality or cost. What you may save in the cost of materials with one system may be traded off against the increased labor or the shorter life of the cover frame.

Perhaps the best compromise is a frame of 3/4-inch EMT (electrical-mechanical tubing), commonly known as conduit. This is a thin-walled, lightweight steel tubing which is used in commercial buildings to house electrical cables. It is available from building supply houses and electrical suppliers, and can be bent with a simple mechanical tubing bender. It is easily cut with an inexpensive tubing cutter.

The actual outside diameter of 3/4-inch conduit is about 7/8 inch. Smaller diameter conduit is cheaper and easier to bend, but lacks the stiffness to span wider boats and support heavy loads. Half-inch conduit might be used for small boats stored in areas where large amounts of snow are not common.

Conduit prices vary significantly, so it pays to shop around. Electrical supply wholesalers that deal primarily with contractors will usually sell to the boatowner if the order is large enough. The frame for a beamy 40-footer might require 400 lineal feet of tubing which should cost no more than about a hundred dollars from a wholesale electrical supplier.

Conduit usually comes in 10-foot lengths, which means that on all but the smallest boats, the transverse frames (like the rafters in a roof) will have to be joined at some point. In order to make the disassembled frames more compact for storage, it is best to make the joint in the transverse frames near the center of each frame. Making the joint slightly off-center makes the attachment of the ridgepole easier. If possible, make only a single bend in any section of conduit. Multiple bends in a single piece are hard to keep in the same plane.

## Joining Conduit

No matter what the material, every cover frame consists of a longitudinal ridgepole, transverse ribs, and on larger frames, longitudinal stringers between the ridgepole and the sides of the boat. If the boat is very wide, or the transverse ribs have a very low pitch, it may be necessary to add upright supports from the deck to the ridgepole to make sure the frame won't collapse under a heavy load of snow.

You can join some parts of your frame with standard conduit fittings, particularly butt (end-to-end) joints such as those required in the long ridgepole. Conduit joined at right angles can

*Kover Klamps offer an easy-to-assemble way of joining conduit at almost any angle.*

be more of a problem. There are several patented connectors such as Kover Klamps (61 Division St., New Rochelle, NY 10801) that are designed to join conduit or tubing at an angle. Kover Klamps are simple to use; only one type of connector is required for various types of joints. Hose clamps or even duct tape can be helpful for joining the conduit in some instances, but these connections are more time-consuming and not as strong as the patented clamps.

## Setting Up the Ridgepole

The first step in building a frame is to decide the height of the ridgepole above the deck. A higher ridgepole does two things: it gives more headroom, and it increases the pitch of the ribs (the transverse framing), which allows the cover to shed snow more easily. The trade-offs are that a higher frame creates more windage, takes more tubing, and requires a larger cover.

The ridgepole should run roughly parallel to the waterline for the middle third or half of the boat. It can then angle down to rest atop the bow and stern railings. You can temporarily support the middle section of the ridgepole with a couple of pieces of conduit or 2x4s lashed together in an X-shaped crutch at the fore and aft ends of the straight section. The angles of the end

*Duct tape can be used for non-critical joints, but it's a nuisance to remove in the spring.*

sections of the ridgepole can be approximated by securing one end of each end section to the bow or stern rail, then overlapping it with the middle section of the ridgepole. Butt joints in the ridgepole and other parts of the frame are made with standard conduit couplings. If you can find them, the rolled steel couplings are stronger than the die-cast ones.

If the ridgepole rests on the bow or stern rail, place padding between the stainless steel rail and the steel conduit to avoid scraping the polished stainless steel surfaces. Add more crutch-type temporary supports as necessary to stabilize the ridgepole, and you're ready to fit the transverse framing.

### Building Transverse Ribs

Begin the transverse framing at the widest part of the boat. You can make the framing on either side of the boat continuous from the deck to the ridgepole, bending the conduit at a height a little above the tops of the stanchions. These ribs can also be made of two pieces, joined with a connector, so that the frame takes up less space when stored for the summer.

Each transverse rib is slightly different from its neighbor. Bending the ribs is therefore a matter of trial and error, cut and fit. The frames should be spaced at intervals of about four feet.

This dimension prevents excessive sagging of the cover between the ribs, which can trap snow and ice. In climates where snow and ice are not a problem, the spacing might be increased to about six feet.

If the conduit ribs are secured to your lifeline stanchions for support, they should be padded and lashed loosely. Otherwise, the constant shifting of the frame as the wind blows against the cover could cause enough movement to break the seal of bedding compound between the stanchion base and the deck, causing leaks. It is better to secure the frame independent of the lifeline stanchions, particularly since the stanchions are probably spaced farther apart than what is ideal for the ribs. You can do this by bending a continuous light batten around the lifeline stanchions from stern to bow just above deck level, then securing the lower ends of the ribs to the batten with U-bolts. You can use 1x2 furring strips for this batten. The batten prevents any of the ribs from moving independently, tying the lower part of your frame together. This gives the frame stability, and keeps it totally separate from the boat's lifeline system, which can even be removed for the winter if you wish.

For wide boats, additional fore-and-aft stringers between the ridgepole and the deck edge will add stability to the frame and reduce pocketing of the cover between the frames. The longitudinals can be made from odds and ends of conduit or pieces of wood furring strip. To reduce the possibility of chafe on the cover, the stringers should be fitted beneath the ribs, not on top of them.

Label all the parts of the frame with an indelible marker, and make a sketch showing the location of each part. Don't count on remembering next year the way the frame went together this year. In subsequent years, reassembly should take no more than an hour or two.

## Preventing Chafe

Inexpensive rubber furniture tips, available at any hardware store, should be fitted to any exposed conduit ends, including the ends of the ribs, the stringers, and the ridgepole. To further reduce the possibility of chafing the cover, all fasteners, clamps, couplers, and U-bolts should point inward, away from the cover.

Tape over these projections if you plan to work on deck over the winter (to reduce the possibility of chafing your head).

When in doubt, pad it. Cheap carpet samples make excellent chafing gear when cut in strips, then taped in place with duct tape at pressure points under the cover. Pressure points occur anywhere the cover must change direction, such as over the ridgepole or at joints in the cover frame.

Whenever possible, tape the chafing gear to itself, rather than to the boat or the frame. The residue of the duct-tape adhesive is difficult to remove from stanchions, pulpits, and gelcoat, and it will pull varnish and paint off any surface it contacts for more than a few minutes.

In addition to preventing the frame from chafing the cover, you must prevent the cover from chafing the boat. Sand or dirt trapped between the cover and the boat will quickly abrade the gelcoat, as will metal grommets if allowed to scrape against the hull. Using a cover that is wide enough to extend below the boot-top on both sides of the boat will help to prevent chafing the topsides. Pulling the cover as tight as possible will reduce its movement on both the frame and the hull, also helping to prevent chafe.

## Tarpaulins

The expected life of a tarp is directly proportional to its cost. The best material for a winter cover is 12-ounce, double-filled cotton duck. This has a dry, fairly soft finish. It will not chafe your hull, nor does it have a waxy finish which will rub off on the boat. Proper care calls for installing it on a well-padded frame to prevent chafe, and storing it carefully in the spring—clean, dry, and protected from insects and rodents. A cover made of 12-ounce cotton duck will last ten years or more. It needs to last, for it costs about fifty cents or more per square foot.

You can also buy lighter weight, dry-finished canvas— usually 10-ounce material. As you might expect, the lighter canvas is cheaper and easier to handle, but won't last as long as the heavier material.

Wax-treated or oil-tempered canvas is cheaper still and equally waterproof, but it can leave a residue on the topsides. The residue is not difficult to remove, however, when the hull is

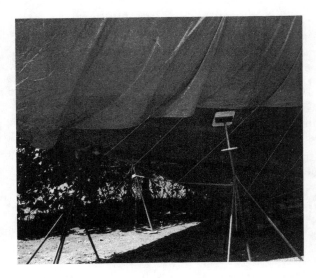

*The tarp should be wide enough to completely cover the topsides, reducing the possibility of chafe.*

cleaned and waxed in the spring. Waxed canvas is stiffer to the touch, but generally drapes well on the frame after a few days in warm sunlight. White or light grey is the best choice of colors to keep the boat cool below the cover and to allow light below for working inside during the winter. The cost of a waxed or oil-tempered tarp is about half that of double-filled canvas.

In recent years, canvas has fallen out of favor due to its cost and weight, and has largely been replaced by polyethylene covers. The ubiquitous bright blue covers which dominate most boatyards are generally made by laminating a woven poly scrim between two layers of ultraviolet-resistant polyethylene sheet.

Poly covers are light, cheap, and strong, but they are not without their disadvantages. Their stiffness and light weight means that they tend to flap and shift on the frame in the lightest breeze, which increases chafe on both the cover and the hull. When the wind picks up, they can make a terrible racket. Unlike canvas, they do not drape particularly well on a frame, and invariably leave wrinkles and pockets that can trap ice and snow.

Polyethylene tarps are light enough, even in the largest sizes, to be handled by one person, making installation easier. Being lighter, they also put less load on the frame, so that the frame need not be as strong. A poly cover 20 feet by 40 feet weighs only about 25 pounds—less than a third the weight of a canvas cover.

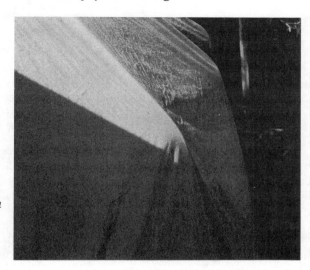

*Pressure points such as the bends in the cover frame can promote chafe and should be padded.*

Poly covers don't rot, and they are less tasty to mice and other small creatures than a good piece of canvas.

Unfortunately, poly covers vary dramatically in quality. Discount stores carry imported poly covers in every size under the sun at prices as low as about five cents per square foot. Better quality polyethylene tarps, made in the U.S., are available at about twice the price of the imports.

If an inexpensive poly cover costs but ten percent of the cost of a good canvas cover, it may make sense to buy one and throw it away every year or two, rather than trying to nurse an expensive canvas cover through ten years.

\*   \*   \*

A conduit frame is simple to build and should last as long as you own your boat. The initial cost may seem high, but it is really quite low when amortized over a number of seasons. A tarpaulin, whether initially expensive or inexpensive, is a bargain considering the years of protection it affords. The wear and tear you save on your boat with the combination of a good, strong frame and a waterproof cover will pay for itself over and over again.

# 8

# Launching and Recommissioning

Springtime commissioning is a whirlwind of activity for most boatowners. As a result, it's not uncommon for one or two important tasks to be overlooked. With that in mind, the prelaunch checklist that follows provides an extensive list of suggestions you'll want to consider before launching.

Some of these suggestions will not be applicable to your boat. In other instances, you might have performed the required maintenance or inspection the previous fall when the boat was decommissioned. In either case, you are fortunate; you can check off those items without even having to get up from your chair.

## A PRELAUNCH CHECKLIST

### Hull Integrity

___ Inspect hoses to all through-hull fittings. What is their condition? Are they routed (where possible) above the waterline to prevent siphoning back into the hull if broken?

___ Inspect all seacocks and gate valves. Inspect, disassemble, and lubricate seacocks. Consider replacing all gate valves with bronze or plastic seacocks.

___ Inspect hose clamps and replace if necessary. Are all hoses below the waterline double clamped? If not, apply additional clamps. (Make sure hose clamps are *all* stainless steel. In many cases, the strap is stainless, but the screw is not.) Consider replacing all snap-on and patented plastic hose clamps with all-stainless steel, screw-tightening clamps.

___ Remove engine stuffing box packing nut and inspect packing. Replace if necessary. Reinstall and tighten packing nut. Also inspect rudder shaft packing if present on your boat and replace if necessary.

___ Check keelbolts for tightness and the attachment area for separation. Repair as indicated.

___ Make sure that hull drain plugs have been installed and tightened properly before launching.

## Rig and Rigging

___ Clean, and wax, varnish, or paint mast as appropriate.

___ Inspect mast for galvanic corrosion where spreaders, winches, or fittings are attached. Repair if present and install gaskets or treat with a corrosion-inhibiting compound.

___ Inspect all standing rigging for general condition, especially at bends or points of strain. Replace any sections demonstrating broken wires.

___ Inspect all turnbuckles and terminals closely. Replace if hairline cracks or galling are evident. Lubricate threads.

___ Inspect running rigging; turn halyards and sheets end-for-end or replace if excessively worn.

___ Inspect and lubricate winches. Check all winch bases and fastenings. Where possible, inspect the laminate under winch bases and backing plates. If stress cracks are evident, reinforce the base area or install larger backing plates.

___Inspect, disassemble and lubricate (where appropriate) all blocks, fairleads, goosenecks, etc.

___Where possible, check chainplates, fastenings, and attachment area. Look for stress cracks.

___Inspect wiring to mast-mounted equipment and test for proper conductance.

___Check radio antennas and masthead instruments for output before installing mast.

___Replace bulbs on mast-mounted lights.

___Inspect the mast step. Repair and reinforce if corrosion or cracking is evident.

___Inspect the mast boot. Reinstall or replace as appropriate.

## General

___Label, diagram and store winter cover framing.

___Clean, fold and store winter cover.

___Check the integrity of lifeline stanchions. Repair as indicated. Check lifelines for broken strands or cracked terminals.

___Check anchors, anchor rodes, and dock lines. Switch anchor rodes and sheets end-for-end to distribute wear.

___Inspect and service anchor windlass if present.

___Install electronics and check for function. Test VHF radios by arrangement with another boat (do not call the Coast Guard for a radio check).

___Inspect and brighten all electrical junctions.

___Inspect and test breakers or fuses. Replace questionable fuses and brighten fuse holders.

___Drain and rinse water tank if anti-freeze was used over the winter. Rinse and fill if left empty.

___Check manual and pressure water pumps for function. Rebuild or replace if faulty.

___Check and update charts. Replace outdated or worn copies.

___Check PFDs for worn spots or rust on fasteners. Replace questionable ones.

___Check life raft, emergency stores ("ditch bag"), and man-overboard gear. Replace items as necessary. Have life raft inspected and repack if indicated.

___Test EPIRB (one second during first five minutes of the hour only), and replace battery if necessary.

___Check distress signaling devices for date and USCG compliance. Add fresh pyrotechnic devices or replace if outdated.

___Check fire extinguishers or Halon system for proper charge; service as indicated.

___Check ship's horn and bell; service or replace if defective.

___Test navigation lights. Clean and apply spray lubricant to connections and sockets wherever possible. Install new bulbs and keep the old ones for spares.

___Check propeller for general condition. Have it reconditioned and polished if appropriate. Grease shaft before reinstalling.

___Replace sacrificial zincs wherever present.

___ Check rudder shaft, tiller head, gudgeons or pintles. Service as indicated.

___ Check wheel steering mechanisms for worn parts, proper cable tension, etc. Lubricate and service as indicated.

___ Analyze spare parts inventory. Bring aboard and catalog.

___ Check sails. Wash, fold, repair, or replace as necessary.

___ Wash and inspect, sail covers, sail bags and spinnaker turtles. Repair or replace if necessary.

___ Inspect, clean and install fenders and fender boards in regular storage places.

___ Check all limber holes in bilge for debris or obstructions.

___ Check bilge pumps, float switches, and strum boxes (strainers). Check for both manual and automatic operations.

___ Inspect boat bottom for early signs of gelcoat blistering. Repair as indicated.

___ Clean and sand boat bottom. Apply bottom paint.

## Cosmetic

___ Inspect hull for scratches, crazing, and oxidation. Polish, wax, repair, or repaint as indicated.

___ Clean, paint or polish and wax (as appropriate) trim detailing and boot-top.

___ Treat rust areas on hull with dilute muriatic acid to remove rust stains. Wear hand and eye protection, and wash well with water afterward.

___Polish and wax all chrome or stainless steel fittings, stanchions, bow pulpits, stern rails, etc. (Dilute muriatic acid can be used to remove rust spots from stainless, but should not be used on chromed brass.)

___Apply varnish to brightwork and treatment to teak trim.

___Remove, wash, and iron cabin curtains.

___Remove, wash, dry, and reinstall canvas covers, dodgers, etc. Inspect, repair, or replace if necessary. Reinforce areas where wear is evident. Lubricate fasteners and replace faulty or missing fasteners.

___Clean and/or vacuum any cabin carpeting.

___Clean and wash lockers and drawers while empty. Repaint if indicated.

___Evaluate accessories (towels, cushions, etc.). Replace or repair if indicated.

___Discard the half bushel of broken, rusted used parts occupying half of the drawer space in the cabin. Utilize the space gained for more practical purposes.

# RECOMMISSIONING THE WINTERIZED ENGINE

___Older gasoline engines (inboard and outboard) should have a complete tune up (spark plugs, points, timing, coil, condenser, distributor cap, etc.). Newer engines with electronic ignitions require little more than new plugs, but be sure to follow manufacturer's recommendations.

___Clean the engine surface; wire brush and repaint rusted areas. (A clean engine not only helps to maintain resale value, it actually encourages more thorough routine maintenance during the season.)

___ Check engine oil; change oil and filter if not changed in the fall at layup.

___ Check transmission lubricant on inboard engines; change if necessary. Drain and refill the lower unit of outboard auxiliary.

___ Clean or replace air filters and intake screens, including the flame arrester screen on the carburetor if applicable.

___ Inspect engine electrical connections for dirt or corrosion and clean as necessary.

___ Oil or lubricate all moving engine parts and engine controls (e.g., carburetor linkages, transmission controls, and so forth).

___ Retension (usually to 1/2-inch deflection) all V-belts eased during lay-up. Inspect for cracks, breaks, or shiny surfaces.

___ Check cooling water intake for barnacles or obstructions.

___ Check thermostat for fouling or corrosion.

___ Reconnect all cooling system hoses, if disconnected before layup. Check all hoses and clamps for deterioration; replace if rusted or cracked.

___ Reinstall water pump impellers if they were removed for storage. (If not removed, keep a careful check on engine temperature when running the engine immediately after launching. Impellers can distort during storage, reducing the volume of water pumped.)

___ Check zinc(s) in cooling system; replace if necessary.

___ Reconnect fuel system plumbing. Check all fuel lines and fittings for cracks or leaks.

___ Fill the fuel tank(s) if they were emptied in the fall.

___ Bleed the fuel lines of air (according to engine manufacturer's directions) if you have a diesel engine.

___ Reinstall batteries, check electrolyte level, and recharge. Clean terminals and connectors to bright metal before installing.

___ Check alternator (or generator) for charging capacity (when engine is run after launching).

___ Check all engine gauges; replace gauge, bulb, or sending unit if defective.

___ Test and lubricate all engine controls.

___ Reconnect the shaft/engine flange, if loosened before layup.

___ Replace the prop, if it was removed for reconditioning during layup.

___ Check cutlass bearings for excessive wear.

___ Check spare parts inventory and replace items as necessary.

___ Remove rag or plug from exhaust outlet.

## LAUNCHING THE TRAILER SAILER

While the responsibility for launching the larger sailboat generally rests with the boatyard, the problems of launching the trailer sailer fall squarely on the shoulders of the owner. In choosing a trailerable sailboat, the sailor is faced with the choice of deep draft or shoal draft. His choice, to a great extent, will determine just what those problems are.

Deeper draft provides better performance and more safety. Reduced draft widens the choice of launching sites and makes trailering and launching easier. The trade-offs can be significant.

Is shoal draft worth the disadvantages? How much does deep draft restrict the trailer sailer?

To help answer these questions, *The Practical Sailor* polled fourteen trailer yacht associations across the United States. We asked each association about the cost, quality, and availability of launching facilities in their sailing areas. What we learned from our study is that deep draft, while it has drawbacks, is not the great restriction that we had been led to believe. Proper trailering equipment can make a significant difference.

## Deep Draft Versus Shoal Draft

When referring to *deep draft,* we mean a boat with a deep, fixed keel. *Shoal draft* denotes a boat with a shorter "stub" keel, or a centerboard or daggerboard which may retract into the hull. A ballasted centerboard that swings back against, but not into the hull, is commonly called a *swing keel.*

The price of decreased draft can be three-fold: you may pay for it in performance, safety, and sometimes in interior space. Boats with a shallow keel are almost always slower to windward than boats with a deep keel. The shallow keel provides less lateral resistance, so the boat makes more leeway. It provides less stability for the same weight, so it must be thicker to carry additional ballast, which increases drag.

A fully retractable daggerboard, centerboard, or swing keel can theoretically offer the performance of a deep, fixed keel. However, the cost of engineering this performance tends to be prohibitive. Holding down the cost means sacrificing other features, like a livable interior.

Safety is a consideration of prime importance to the sailor

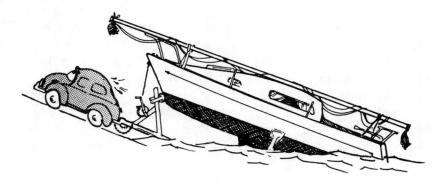

who plans to venture into open waters. Swing keels and center-boards on trailerable sailboats rarely have provision to be locked in the down position. In a capsize, the centerboard can retract into its trunk, encouraging the boat to turn turtle (upside down). Similarly, should the centerboard's pivot pin shear off, the boat could be rendered very unstable.

Finally, interior space is lost to the centerboard or dagger-board trunk in boats with fully retracting boards, and the cabin may be awkwardly divided by the trunk.

These compromises make a boat with a deep keel look particularly attractive. The aforementioned trade-off is in the difficulty of launching such a boat. The hull of a boat with a deep keel sits high above the trailer, so the trailer has to be pushed into deeper water before the boat will float off. On a steep, paved launching ramp this might not pose a problem, but on a more gradual ramp of soft dirt, launching might be impossible. Of course, you can always launch a deep keel sailboat with a hoist, but there are fewer hoists in operation than there are launching ramps, and their use is much more expensive.

## Hoists: How Many and How Much?

If hoists were as abundant and inexpensive as launching ramps, there would be a lot more deep draft sailboats on trailers. Unfortunately, hoists are neither abundant nor cheap. Our questionnaires report 604 hoists available for public launching, compared to 2155 launching ramps.

Hoists are more common in some areas than in others. Questionnaires from metropolitan areas of California list half as many hoists as ramps; areas on the Great Lakes list nearly equal numbers of hoists and ramps. By contrast, questionnaires from more rural areas indicate hoists are few and far between.

Launching by hoist or mobile lift is not cheap. Reported charges range from $2 to $5 a foot per launching, which comes to $40 to $100 to launch a 20-foot sailboat. Annual fees at sailing clubs, which often include use of a hoist, are more reasonable; they range as low as $75 a year. Many sailing clubs and marinas offer dry-sailing: space on land to store the boat between sails. Unless your boat is used primarily for racing against other members of the club, sailing out of a club effectively defeats the purpose of owning a trailerable sailboat—you're stuck in one sailing area.

If your boat must be launched by hoist, the same reasoning applies. One of the major reasons for owning a trailerable sailboat is to be able to travel to new sailing waters, but if you plan to travel to less populated areas, the choice will be limited by the dearth of suitable launching facilities.

## Condition of Launching Ramps

How many launching ramps are steep enough and well-paved enough to launch a deep-keel boat? How hard is it to use them?

As might be expected, launching a deep-keel boat is deemed a lot harder than launching a boat of shoal draft. What sounds more discouraging is that, with a conventional trailer and hitch, only about ten percent of the launching ramps reportedly could accommodate a small boat with a deep keel under the best conditions. "Best conditions" means high tide or high water. If high tide occurs at noon and you go for an afternoon sail, you might not be able to get back on the trailer until well after dark. Likewise, sailing on a lake could be restricted to times of high water in the spring and early summer.

This problem, however, sounds worse than it is. About half of the ramps will accommodate deep draft boats if the distance between the boat and the hauling vehicle is increased to get the boat and trailer into deeper water.

There are two ways to increase that distance: use a trailer with an extendable tongue, or detach the tongue from the car or truck. The second option requires using a chain between the trailer and the vehicle, supporting the tongue of the trailer with a large diameter wheel, and pushing the trailer into the water.

While the number of ramps suitable for deep draft boats seems highly restrictive, the use of an extension on the trailer increases the number so much that, when combined with the available hoists, deep draft boats could be an acceptable option to many sailors.

An extension is useful to owners of shoal draft boats, as well. A swing keel or stub keel boat can be launched with no extension from about half the ramps in our study. Using an extension makes almost ninety percent of the ramps usable.

A sailboat with a fully retractable centerboard or dagger-board can be launched at most ramps. Extending the trailer allows access to a few more ramps of marginal slope, but the difference would not justify the extra expense in most situations.

## Some Common Launching Problems

We asked the trailer yacht associations to identify problems commonly encountered while launching a trailerable boat. Here is what they reported:

**DOCKAGE.** Dockage at launching ramps is too often inadequate or non-existent. Often docks can only be found during the summer. During the spring and fall, when the water is coldest, you must get wet to get the boat on and off the trailer, and hang on to it while someone parks the car and then climbs aboard.

**LONG WAITS.** Respondents report that on a busy summer day, waits of up to 45 minutes are common at public launching ramps. Many owners complain that others waste ramp time by putting up the mast on the ramp instead of beforehand in the parking lot.

**POWER LINES.** Despite a number of deaths in recent years, a surprising number of ramps still have power lines running overhead nearby. One report notes that contact with power lines has caused six dismastings at one club in the past eight years.

**BRIDGES.** Bridges sometimes block access to open water, a problem most common in southern California. A mast which is hinged on deck can be tilted back to clear an overhead obstruction, but with a keel-stepped mast, you could be stuck.

**MANEUVERING ONTO THE TRAILER.** Respondents were nearly unanimous in condemning "powerboat-style" trailers where the boat is winched onto the trailer over a series of rollers. Superior for a sailboat is a "float-on" trailer with well-padded keel guides, padded bunks and a bow stop. A float-on trailer with proper guides will allow sailing the boat onto the trailer even in a strong crosswind or cross current, although extra caution is required in such conditions, especially if there is any wave action. A sailboat positioned improperly on its trailer supports is liable to sustain serious damage.

**TRAILER JACKS.** Trailer jacks are intended to be used to lift the trailer's tongue off the trailer hitch. If the jack has a wheel, it is usually too small to be used for anything but wheeling the boat around on level pavement. It should not be used as a third wheel to launch a boat; it will invariably get bogged down in the sand or muck at the bottom of a launching ramp. If you plan to use a third wheel and chain, instead of an extendable tongue, get a separate wheel, preferably with an inflatable tire.

**PARKING LOT SECURITY.** The best launching ramps have secure, well-lit parking lots. Those located in parks with park wardens on all-night duty are preferred.

*     *     *

Some owners take full advantage of the mobility of the trailer-able boat to explore new cruising grounds or to race against new competition. For others, the difficulties of launching and hauling quickly outweigh the advantage of mobility. Many trailer-boat owners eventually resort to paying for both a slip in a marina for the boat, and a space in a storage yard for the trailer.

Even with a fixed keel of moderate draft, a trailerable sailboat can be the answer to crowded marinas and high mooring or slip-rental fees. Hauling and launching a trailerable sailboat requires, however, that the owner deal with some special considerations: The weight of the boat and trailer must be matched to an appropriate towing vehicle, and the equipment must be matched to the local launching options as well as the owner's tolerance for launching hassles.

# TUNING THE MASTHEAD RIG

Most of us—whether daysailors, racers, or cruisers—value good performance. We like our boats to sail reasonably fast, and we like the helm to be light and responsive.

Tuning the rig of a boat is one of the necessary—and pleasant—tasks which must be done to achieve good performance. In an untuned boat, the mast bends in odd ways, and this in turn causes the sails to set badly. By contrast, on a well-tuned boat, the rig bends in a controlled fashion, allowing the sails to do their best. For this reason, an avid racer will be constantly fiddling with the tune of his boat, while for most of us a one-time job during commissioning may suffice.

The first thing to realize is that for a mast to stand well, it should not be straight when in a static, no load situation. This was something that some sailors realized thirty years ago when the conventional advice was to tune rigs so that masts were indeed straight when static. While that advice is still sometimes given, most of the sailing world has realized that a controlled static bend is needed.

The problem with a statically straight mast is that when it is loaded, it is too easy for the mast to invert, or bend backwards (**Figure 8-1**). This can happen when the boat is beating in a seaway or reaching with a spinnaker. Most mast sections can accommodate a significant amount of forward bend without failure, but very little aft bend.

With a poorly tuned rig, each time the boat comes off a wave, the mast will pump and wriggle so much that you can actually see it changing shape from the cockpit. When this happens there is a real danger of losing the rig. In contrast, if you set up the rig so that it has "prebend", that is, the center of the mast bends forward when in a static condition, the loaded mast will flex in the proper direction. What flex there is will then tend to flatten the main, rather than causing it to develop excessive draft, and the boat should balance better, particularly in heavy air, when most boats start to develop helm problems.

The first job is to get the mast straight athwartships. Leave the lower shrouds hand-tight during this procedure. Use the main halyard to take measurements. Take the shackled end of the halyard a measured distance aft of the bow along the gunwale, then have someone take up the slack while you hold the shackle firmly to that point. Cleat off the halyard. Then take the end of the halyard to the same point on the other side of the boat. If the mast is straight athwartships, the halyard shackle will just kiss the same point on the gunwale on either side of the boat.

Because chainplates are rarely perfectly symmetrical from one side of the boat to the other, it is best to go to the trouble to measure back from the stemhead on each side for your reference mark, rather than using the chainplates as the reference.

If the halyard does not touch the same point on both sides of the boat, adjust the capshrouds (upper shrouds) until the mast is straight. Be sure to loosen one side as you tighten the other, and sight up the mast to make sure that you haven't put any sideways bend in. The sailtrack should be straight athwartships when you sight up the mast (unless it has been put on crooked).

It should be noted if your deck is slightly crooked (a fairly common problem) the mast may not be perfectly centered athwartships in the partners when it is vertical to the hull. Don't attempt to make the mast vertical by putting a level on the side of the mast. Almost no boat floats without a list to one side or the other, and your weight alone is enough to effect a slight list, even on a fairly large boat.

At this point, on boats up to about thirty-five feet, the capshroud turnbuckles should be hand-tight (as tight as you can get a well-lubricated turnbuckle with your bare hands). Later, when testing under sail, you will find the leeward shrouds slopping around by a few inches; then, and only then, you can take the slack out of the leeward shrouds. If you have absolutely no slack in the leeward capshroud when the boat is going upwind in 12 knots of wind, the shrouds are probably too tight for most boats.

Next set the rake of the mast using the forestay and backstay, again only hand tight. If you don't know from experience what the proper rake should be, begin with a modest rake of no more than the fore and aft diameter of the mast. Use the main halyard as a plumb bob. Later you may wish to modify this rake. Utilize the fact that increasing the mast rake or moving the mast aft increases weather helm, while decreasing mast rake or moving the mast forward decreases weather helm. Now that the mast is straight athwartships and properly raked, it's time to start the controlled bends. These are accomplished with the forward lowers, babystay, backstay, and mast wedges. Whether your boat has double forward lowers or a single centerline babystay does not matter. Both systems accomplish the same end.

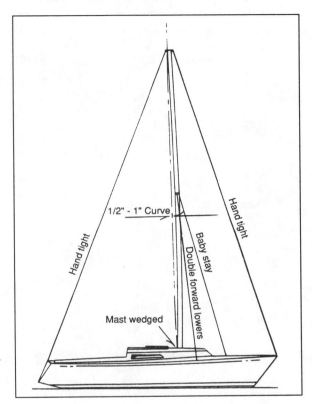

*Figure 8-1.* Pre-bend the mast slightly before loading the headstay and backstay.

First, take up the babystay or double forward lowers until you have pulled a forward bend of half an inch to an inch into the middle section of the mast (**Figure 8-1**). Again use the main halyard, pulled tight against the lower, aft edge of the mast, as a measuring reference. If using double lowers, make sure the mast remains straight athwartships.

Next, crank up on the backstay until you have a curve in the mast equal to one-half to one times the fore and aft dimensions of the mast (**Figure 8-2**). Finally, take up the aft lowers hand tight.

If your mast is stepped on the keel, at this point you need to wedge it at the partners. Wooden wedges are the easiest to make, but they can dent an aluminum mast if the shrouds are set so loosely that the mast leans to leeward significantly when sailing upwind. A fairly firm rubber wedge works better with looser

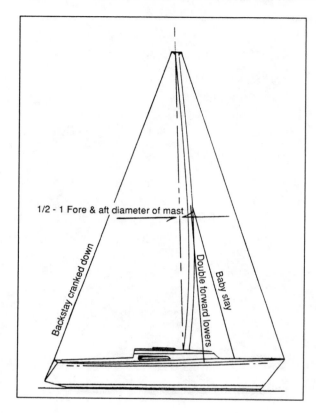

1/2 - 1 Fore & aft diameter of mast

Backstay cranked down

Double forward lowers

Baby stay

*Figure 8-2. The full amount of pre-bend won't be apparent until the backstay and headstay are fully loaded.*

rigs, and is probably the safest to use. Rubber wedges are usually harder to make, however.

Your boatyard or chandlery may sell special rubber for mast wedges. If not, try to buy something in the nature of a thick innertube. In a pinch, sections cut from auto tires will do, but will have to be rasped to thickness. Don't use a foam material; it's too soft. You will need two wedges, one forward, one aft. The width of each should be about 35 percent to 40 percent of the mast's circumference. Thus, they will curve around both the front and sides of the mast. Since the rubber wedges must be under compression, their thickness should be slightly greater than the gap they need to fill. You may have to cement together several layers of thin rubber to achieve the proper thicknesses.

The first step in wedging is to trim the wedges so they do not

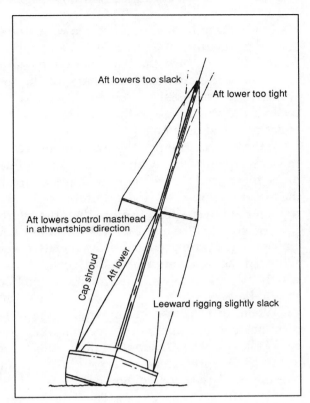

Aft lowers too slack

Aft lower too tight

Aft lowers control masthead
in athwartships direction

Cap shroud

Aft lower

Leeward rigging slightly slack

*Figure 8-3. The
mast must be
checked for
straightness when
sailing upwind.
Fine tuning may be
required here.*

push the mast out of column sideways. As noted earlier, many
decks are slightly off center, so there may not be equal space on
both sides of the mast, even when it is in the proper position.

When the wedges are properly trimmed for the sides of the
partners, you are ready to insert the aft wedge. To support the
prebend, put a line around the mast a foot or so above the
partners, and run it forward to a fixed point (a snatch block on a
mooring cleat or a bridle between the cleats) then aft to a cockpit
winch. Now slip the aft wedge into place. Release the load on the
line, and insert the forward wedge. A little soap on the wedge
will ease a tight fit.

Now you're ready for a sailing trial. Choose a day when you
can comfortably carry a genoa. About 8 to 15 knots of wind will
do for most boats.

Put the boat hard and full on the wind and check the mast. It should be retaining the same fore and aft curve you put in while tuning. If not, adjust the babystay or forward lower shrouds. Next check the athwartships shape of the mast. It should be straight. Any necessary adjustments should be carried out with the leeward shrouds, then the boat should be tacked to check the effect of the adjustments.

If the mast is straight athwartships, tack and hand-tighten all the leeward shrouds by an equal number of turns. If the center of the mast bends to weather, tighten the capshrouds more than the lowers (**Figure 8-3**). If the center of the mast sags to leeward, tighten the lower shrouds more than the capshrouds.

You should also check the athwartships bend of the mast in varying wind strengths, adjusting the aft lowers until you have achieved the best compromise between a straight mast and one which falls off or hooks. A masthead which hooks to windward should be avoided.

When, after a few sailing trials, you're satisfied, pin the turnbuckles, then tape everything that could catch a sail or sheet.

We have dealt with what might be called traditionally rigged masts, those with spreaders at roughly right angles to the mast. Nothing we have covered, however, is not also true of fractional rigs with aft-raking spreaders. The only difference is that on such a rig the capshrouds, as they load up, work on the spreaders to increase forward mast bend—but that's all to the better.

## STORM SURVIVAL IN PORT

Having begun Part II of this volume with the statement that the responsibilities of boat ownership don't end when the boat is decommissioned, it seems logical to conclude with a review of the responsibilities that do begin when the boat is commissioned or recommissioned.

It is not our intention to lecture the boatowner on his duties and obligations to his boat, or to complain that boatyard and marina personnel cannot be depended upon to assume those responsibilities. Rather it is our intention to remind the boatowner that once the boat is in commission, he must give at least as much attention to preparations for heavy weather in port as his insurer will in the event of a damage claim.

Modern forecasting methods are far from perfect, but storms are almost always tracked with enough precision to let you know if you are in the path of potential destruction. With a day or more of warning, there are many precautions you can take to give your boat the best chance of survival.

## Reduce Windage

When the load exerted on a boat's ground tackle—whether a mooring or her own anchors—exceeds the holding power of the ground tackle, the boat will drag. One of the primary contributors to that load is the windage of the boat.

When a boat lies perfectly head to wind, windage is relatively small, consisting of the frontal area of the hull, deck structures, spars, and rigging. Rarely, however, does a boat lie perfectly head to wind through a storm. Instead, the boat yaws from side to side as it sails around on its anchors or mooring. The total area presented to the wind, and hence, the total loading on the ground tackle, varies dramatically. The area presented by a boat broadside to the wind is several times that presented by the same boat when it is perfectly head to wind. Since the change in wind loading is a function of the square of the wind velocity, the strain on ground tackle varies geometrically as the boat yaws. Reducing windage will help to reduce the total loading, and help the boat to stay put.

You can substantially reduce the windage of any boat with only a few hours of work. First, remove Bimini tops, cockpit dodgers, spray curtains around cockpits, and awnings. These are pretty obvious; the rest may not be.

Roller furling headsails should be struck and stored ashore or below. The windage of a rolled-up sail is significant, but the real danger comes if the sail unfurls, as it almost always will, no matter how well tied it may be. Mainsails should be removed for the same reason. If the sail is so big that you can't handle it yourself, and you have no one to help, add extra sail ties, and thoroughly and tightly lash down the sail cover. The normal securing system consisting of sail ties and sail cover is not adequate to hold the sail in place during a major storm. If the sail gets loose, it will certainly destroy itself; at worst, it will add enough windage to make the boat drag its ground tackle.

Take off man-overboard gear, cockpit cushions, cowl vents, antennas, and even halyards if they can be replaced easily. Internal halyards can be run to the masthead, leaving a single halyard led to deck to allow you to retrieve the others after the storm. Halyards can add a great deal of windage, and no matter how well you tie them off, will invariably flog the daylights out of your spars. Likewise, masthead instruments, particularly anemometer cups, may simply blow away.

## Get It Off the Boat

It's a good idea to take everything that is not bolted down off the boat entirely. If a boat does go ashore, it's a sad fact that vandals may make short work of her. Electronics, clocks, barometers, books, navigation gear may all vanish. If you value it, take it off the boat. Chances are that no insurance policy will cover you well enough to make up for the loss of valuable gear.

## Know Your Ground Tackle

Is your mooring really a 1000-pound mushroom anchor, or is it simply a chunk of concrete or an old engine block? It may be worth a dive to the bottom to find out, preferably before a storm threatens. Likewise, all shackles, chains, and mooring pennants should be examined at least once a season to make sure they are of adequate size and in good shape. If the condition of any component of the system is questionable, replace it. If an insurance adjuster sees a corroded piece of chain or a mooring pennant that is badly worn, he may be reluctant to approve your claim in case of loss.

In crowded harbors, permanent moorings may lack adequate scope to deal with the high tides associated with storm conditions. It may be possible to increase the scope for a storm by replacing or lengthening the mooring pennant. The holding power of a permanent mooring is increased by additional scope just as it is with an anchor.

Some moorings are equipped with large, inflatable surface buoys. The positive flotation of these buoys may reduce the holding power of the mooring in extremely high tides, so it may be worth removing the buoy before a storm, Just don't forget to replace it before casting off the mooring pennant after the storm is over.

## At the Dock

As a rule, boats tied to docks are at greater risk than boats kept on moorings or at anchor. Floating docks are rarely strong enough to take the loads exerted on them by boats in storm conditions. In addition, if the tides are extremely high, floating docks may simply float off the pilings which hold them in place.

A boat kept at a dock can't swing to face into the wind as storm winds change direction. Therefore, the boat at a dock almost always presents more windage than a boat lying at anchor that is free to swing head to wind.

If your boat must be kept at a dock in a storm, secure the lines to pilings, rather than to floating docks. It is best to tie the lines high on the pilings, so they will not be chafed if floating docks ride up on the pilings. Instead of using loose bowlines around the pilings, use multiple clove hitches, or a clove hitch finished with two half-hitches. That way, the lines will tighten on the pilings, and are unlikely to pull off even if the water rises above the pilings.

## Anchored Out

If you have good ground tackle or a good mooring, your boat may be safer anchored out than tied to a dock. You won't have to worry about crashing into docks, or docks crashing into you. What you will have to be concerned about is other boats with less adequate ground tackle dragging down on you, either damaging your boat or straining your own ground tackle so much that your boat drags.

The first rule of thumb when anchored or moored during a severe storm is to get out as much ground tackle as possible. You may have a good permanent mooring, but if you back it up with your own anchors, you are going to have an even better chance of survival.

Usually, it is possible to forecast the likely direction of the strongest winds, even with a storm whose exact path is unknown. A good rule of thumb is to deploy your heaviest anchor in the expected direction of the strongest winds, and your second anchor 180 degrees from that. You may want to put your primary anchor upwind of and at a 45-degree angle to the mooring, so there will be less likelihood of chafe between your anchor rode and your mooring chain.

When putting out your anchors, get them as far from the boat as your rodes will allow, leaving perhaps twenty-five feet of line on deck to make adjustments after the anchors are down. The more scope you have out on the anchors, the better they will hold. All anchors hold best when the pull on them is perfectly horizontal. You may increase the holding power of an anchor by 25 percent by increasing the scope from 5:1 to 10:1.

Remember that your biggest anchor may not necessarily be the one with most holding power in a particular bottom. If you are anchored in soft mud, a Danforth will have much more holding power than a kedge anchor of the same weight.

## Prevent Chafe

Line chafe has probably caused the loss of more boats than any other single factor. Whether you are on a mooring or at the dock, your lines must be protected from chafe. No matter how well polished your bow chocks are, they are still metal, and are harder than your lines. In a storm lasting several hours, even the smoothest metal fittings will start to wear away your lines.

Chafing gear can be made from almost any material. Canvas and leather are the traditional materials used, but dacron sail-repair tape or even old towels or T-shirts will do. Old denim blue jeans cut in strips make exceptionally good chafing gear.

Chafing gear will not do any good if it does not stay in place. The best chafing gear is leather sewn over the lines, but if you are preparing for a storm, it's too late to be elegant. Duct tape—and plenty of it—will do in a pinch. You can also tie the chafing gear on with light nylon line, but it too, is subject to chafe.

Chafing gear should cover more of the line than you think will come into contact with a chafing hazard, to allow for fine tuning the lines, to compensate for stretch, and to make up for the fact that the chafing gear may slip under load. In addition, if you are aboard your boat during a storm, you may want to ease out a foot of line now and then to shift the location of chafe slightly.

# Double Up Lines

Whenever possible, dock lines and mooring pennants should be doubled. If one fails, you want a backup. The only danger here is that the deck can quickly become a rat's nest. In addition, those elegant little cleats may suddenly be too small to take two 3/4-inch dock lines. It is almost impossible to have cleats that are too large, or anchors that are too big.

Whenever possible, lead heavily loaded lines to winches before belaying them on cleats. Winches are likely to have more fastenings, distributing their load over a larger area of the deck. Distributing the loads between a winch and a cleat can be a tricky business. Normally, when using a winch you take three turns around it, so that almost all the load is carried by the winch. Using only one or two turns on the winch allows more load to be carried by the cleat.

Don't carry several heavily loaded lines to a single cleat. That's like putting all your eggs in one basket. If the cleat goes, the boat goes. This is when multiple cleats on the bow pay off. You can lead each anchor or mooring line to a separate cleat, not only making it easier to adjust individual lines, but distributing the load better.

Through-bolted cleats are designed to be loaded in sheer; that is, with the load parallel to the deck and perpendicular to the cleat's fasteners. When the load becomes a tension load—vertical to the fastenings—you're headed for trouble. Watch the lead of lines carefully in order to load hardware properly. Sometimes, a strong snatch block can be used to deflect loading to a better angle, or to reduce chafe. For storm-induced loads, don't use a block to change a lead more than about 45 degrees. You are likely to induce loads on the block or its point of attachment that it just can't handle.

Lines can pop out of open bow chocks as the boat pitches. It may be possible to lash lines into chocks by passing a light line under the bow or to adjacent hardware. Closed chocks or hawseholes can prevent this problem, but once again, you must watch the direction of loading. Closed chocks are designed to be loaded downward, not upward. If you put a tension load on the chock's fastenings, they may pull out of the deck or toerail.

The need for strength in deck hardware is obvious, but the

strength of a particular installation is not always so obvious. Without proper backing plates, adequate-sized through-bolts, and a strong attachment area, the strength of any piece of deck hardware is compromised. Commissioning time is the best time to crawl around under the deck to check these things out. You'll sleep easier and thus enjoy your boat more knowing that heavily loaded hardware is securely attached.

### Hauling Out

Usually, boatyards are overwhelmed with frantic calls from owners to haul their boats before a major storm. Hauling may or may not be a good idea. Hauling a boat and leaving the mast in is an invitation to disaster. Hauling at a yard that is only a few feet above water level also may gain little. Putting the boat inside a shed that blows down is no help at all.

By all means, if your boat is trailerable, get it out of the water. Tow it to high ground, and don't park it under a tree!

### On or Off the Boat?

If your boat is on an anchor or mooring, you may increase its chances of survival by staying on the boat. You may be able to fend off a boat that is dragging its anchor, adjust a critical line, or take the load of the ground tackle by running the engine. You also increase your chances of serious injury. Boats are replaceable; people are not.

There is no easy answer to this question. Few experiences are more heartbreaking than watching another boat chafe through your anchor lines while you are helpless on the shore, but few are more terrifying than being aboard a boat that is dragging down to destruction on a concrete seawall that towers over your head.

### Should You Move Your Boat?

One of the most basic questions is whether your boat should be moved to another harbor. Most regions have protected anchorages known as hurricane holes. The problem is that these are usually known to everyone, and may become so crowded when a major storm threatens as to become more dangerous than a more exposed anchorage.

Moving to a hurricane hole early is no guarantee of safety. You may get the best spot, but there is no way to keep someone from anchoring right on top of you. If you think boatowners are a generous and gentlemanly bunch, you haven't seen them in times of stress when their boats are endangered.

You must realistically assess your chances for survival wherever you are. If strong southerlies are forecast in a harbor whose north end is a stone wall, you had better think about moving elsewhere, or at least moving as close under the weather shore as is practical. Don't forget to allow for changes in wind direction, however.

The wind itself is usually less of a problem than high tides and waves which reduce scope and increase chafe as the boat surges. If you are behind a seawall which is only five feet above mean high water, a storm which comes at high tide is likely to submerge the breakwater, exposing you to the full force of wind and waves.

Try to imagine what will happen to docks, pilings, seawalls, and the other boats around you. What happens when the wind shifts? What if the docks come loose? Don't move your boat until you have a coherent plan, and only if you can say with confidence that the place you have chosen is better than the place you are. An exposed location with a bottom that has good holding characteristics may be better than a protected location with poor holding, assuming that you have adequate ground tackle.

If possible, try to stay close to the boat during the storm, as long as you don't risk your life. If your boat does come ashore, you may be able to reduce the damage or prevent vandalism if you are close at hand. And finally, if possible, take photographs of your storm preparations. If your insurance company questions a claim on your boat, it may help to have pictures of how you have prepared her.

*       *       *

If you have done all you can to secure the boat—reducing windage, removing valuable gear, putting out extra lines or anchors, adding chafing gear—you have done all that can be expected to prepare your boat to meet a storm in port. Get off the boat and seek shelter with a clear conscience.

Boats, unfortunately, are sometimes lost despite the best efforts of the owner. No amount of preparation will save your boat if the forces of nature and the laws of chance conspire against her. While the sailor can exercise no control over the weather, he can, at times, make his own luck. Careful storm preparation will not guarantee your boat's survival, but it will ensure that the odds are always in your favor.

# Index